Country Cooking

T I M E - L I F E   B O O K S

Alexandria, Virginia

Country Cooking

recipes for traditional country fare

A REBUS BOOK

CONTENTS

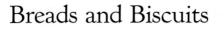

Breads and Biscuits

*quick breads, yeast breads, popovers, sopaipillas, as
well as traditional biscuits · regional specialties · a feature
on shaped breads*

Desserts

*cakes, pies, puddings, ice creams, a fool, a crisp, and
a cobbler · regional specialties · features on festive drinks,
decorative pie crusts, and pitters and seeders*

CREDITS

INDEX

American country cooking. The words immediately conjure up thoughts of a kitchen filled with the tantalizing aroma of baking bread, of soups bubbling in heavy stockpots, of apple pie, fried chicken, and Boston baked beans . . . of mom and grandma. Country-style cooking not only expresses down-home warmth but also re-creates a bit of the past. Indeed many of the recipes in this book have been handed down for generations.

In the early days of this country, when most foods were scarce and cooking equipment limited, cooks had to be clever in order not to starve; often, corn and beans were the only foods the early colonists had to eat. Later their diet improved with the addition of a greater variety of vegetables, meats, fish, game, and poultry, but life was still no picnic. All cooking was done at the hearth and foods often simmered for hours as the housewife tended to her many other duties. In those days cookbooks did not exist, and methods of cooking were usually passed on through word of mouth or as handwritten "receipts." It was not until 1796 that the first American cookbook, Amelia Simmons's *American Cookery,* was published, giving directions for such dishes as Indian pudding, watermelon pickles, and johnnycakes.

While a number of the recipes in this volume date back to the earliest days of the colonies, others originated later with the immigrant groups who settled in various parts of the country and contributed to America's "melting pot" cuisine. When William Penn established his colony outside Philadelphia in 1682, for example, huge numbers of German Protestants began to arrive, and we have them to thank for such dishes as hot potato salad, fried tomatoes, and chicken corn soup with noodles. Similarly, when immigrants from France, Canada, and the Caribbean began settling the Mississippi delta in the early 18th century, Louisiana Creole and Cajun cooking came into being. Among the recipes in this book are such well-known Louisiana specialties as jambalaya, maque choux, and red beans and rice.

It is these and many other traditional regional and ethnic dishes that are at the heart of country cooking. But today's country cooking is not necessarily old-fashioned. Where once soups and stews required long cooking, many of those in this book have had their cooking times trimmed. Where the original recipes used tubs of lard and endless eggs, these modern interpretations have been lightened to appeal to the contemporary palate. None, however, lose the richness of flavor that is so essential to fine country food.

As you look through this book you will find ideas not only for simple and elegant country breakfasts, lunches, and dinners, but also for pretty tableware and creative centerpieces. For as good as country food is, somehow it tastes even better when presented in a charming country setting.

Soups and Chowders

*perfect with a glass of wine
and a loaf of crusty bread*

Whether a satisfying main dish or an elegant first course, soups and chowders are a traditional mainstay of the country table. Served hot, a soup can take the bite out of a cold winter day; served chilled, it is an ideal refresher on a steamy summer afternoon.

In early America, soups were an amalgam of what was on hand: mainly game, wild birds, and seafood, with fresh vegetables tossed in during the summer. In New England, for instance, chowders became standard fare because seafood was plentiful; in Pennsylvania, the Germans favored hearty soups with dumplings; in the coastal South, bisques featured crabs and crawfish; and throughout the country, bean soups were the thrifty cook's saving grace.

This chapter not only offers favorite recipes for soups and chowders from many regions of the country, but also features contemporary recipes, such as Plum Tomato Soup and Fresh Pea Soup, that take advantage of the bounty of the garden.

The makings for an elegant Southern Shrimp Bisque.

Light Corn Chowder

This corn chowder is lighter and fresher tasting than its traditional counterpart, which is considerably starchier. If you'd prefer a thicker chowder, purée one-third of the solids at the end of Step 4, and stir the purée back into the soup.

¼ pound bacon (4 to 6 slices)
1 medium onion, chopped (about 1¼ cups)
¼ cup flour
2 cups canned chicken broth
1 cup water
3 cups peeled and diced (½ inch) yams (about ¾ pound)
½ teaspoon thyme

2½ cups corn kernels, fresh (about 5 large ears), or frozen, thawed
1 medium red bell pepper, cut into ½-inch dice (about 1 cup)
1 medium zucchini (about ¼ pound), cut into ½-inch dice (about 1 cup)
1 cup milk
2 tablespoons chopped parsley

1. In a 3- to 4-quart saucepan or soup pot, cook the bacon over medium heat until crisp, 8 to 10 minutes. Reserving the fat in the pan, drain the bacon on paper towels; crumble and set aside.

2. Add the onion to the pan and sauté over medium heat until softened but not browned, about 10 minutes. Increase the heat to medium-high, stir in the flour and cook, stirring constantly, for 1 minute.

3. Add the chicken broth, water, yams, and thyme, and bring to a boil. Reduce the heat to medium-low, cover, and simmer until the yams are tender, about 15 minutes.

4. Add the corn, red pepper, zucchini, and milk. Return to a simmer and cook until the corn is just tender, 1 to 2 minutes.

5. Sprinkle the chowder with the bacon and parsley, and serve hot.   *6 servings*

Light Corn Chowder

Clam and Scallop Chowder

Thick fish soups, or chowders, have been a staple of coastal New England cookery since the early 1700s. Chowders were originally thickened only with common crackers (hard, crisp wheat-flour crackers similar in nature to oyster crackers), but their role was taken over by the potato when it became commercially available in the late 18th century. In this variation on a New England clam chowder, both crackers and potatoes are used. For an even richer chowder, stir ½ cup of heavy cream into the soup just before serving.

3 dozen little neck or cherrystone clams, scrubbed
8 unsalted saltine crackers, crushed
2½ cups milk
¼ pound salt pork, diced
2 cups water
2 tablespoons butter
1 cup chopped shallots (about 8 medium), or 1 cup chopped onion

1 clove garlic, minced
2 tablespoons flour
1 pound red potatoes, peeled and diced (about 2½ cups)
1 bay leaf
¼ cup chopped fresh dill
½ pound bay scallops or quartered sea scallops
¼ teaspoon cracked pepper

1. Discard any clams whose shells are open (tap open shells first; if they close, the clams are still alive and can be used). Place the clams in a large pot of water and soak for 30 minutes. Rinse the clams well in 4 changes of water.

2. In a small bowl, combine the crackers and milk, and set aside to soak.

3. In a small saucepan of boiling water, blanch the salt pork for 5 minutes. Drain well, pat dry, and set aside.

4. Place the clams in a large saucepan. Add the 2 cups water, cover, and steam over high heat until the shells open, about 5 minutes. With a slotted spoon, remove the clams, cover loosely with aluminum foil, and set aside. Strain the cooking liquid through a sieve lined with a double thickness of dampened cheesecloth and set aside.

5. In a soup pot or large saucepan, melt the butter over medium-high heat. Add the salt pork, shallots, and garlic, and cook, stirring, until the shallots are softened but not browned, 5 to 8 minutes. Stir in the flour and cook, stirring constantly, for 1 minute.

6. Add the potatoes and bay leaf, reduce the heat to medium-low, cover, and cook until the potatoes are tender, 10 to 15 minutes.

7. Meanwhile, remove the clam meat from the shells, chop, and set aside, loosely covered.

8. When the potatoes are tender, gradually stir in the reserved clam broth and bring to a boil. Stir in 2 tablespoons of the dill, the crackers, and milk. Return to a boil, add the scallops, and cook for 30 seconds. Add the chopped clams and stir briefly to heat through.

9. Discard the bay leaf. Sprinkle the soup with the pepper and the remaining 2 tablespoons dill, and serve hot.   *4 to 6 servings*

Hardshell clams, or quahogs, are harvested on the East Coast and shipped throughout this country. The smallest quahogs are called little necks; the medium-size ones are referred to as cherrystones; and the largest (often toughest) clams are known as chowder clams because they benefit from being simmered in a chowder or other soup.

Vegetable-Beef Soup with Barley

Old-fashioned soups such as this one are made for the back burner: beef bones, a handful of aromatic vegetables, and water are put into a heavy stockpot early in the morning and allowed to cook all day to make a flavorful soup base. Although this recipe takes about twelve hours from start to finish (which includes six hours of refrigeration time; see Step 4), the cooking time can be shortened, if desired, by substituting four cups of canned beef broth for four cups of the water used to make the stock. This will strengthen the stock and allow you to halve the cooking time in Step 2.

Barley not only provides interesting texture and body to soup, it also makes a tasty base for a nourishing grain salad. To make a barley salad, "cook" the barley by simply steeping, or soaking, it: Add ½ cup of boiling water for each cup of the grain, and let the barley soak for half an hour. It will become tender but chewy and, when drained, is delicious combined with chopped raw vegetables and a tangy dressing.

2 large beef shanks (about 2 pounds total)
1 pound veal bones (optional)
12 cups water
2 medium onions, whole and unpeeled
2 medium carrots, whole and unpeeled
2 stalks celery
2 teaspoons salt
1 bay leaf
½ teaspoon marjoram
½ teaspoon basil
6 peppercorns

½ cup pearl barley
4 small white turnips (about ½ pound), peeled, cut into ¼-inch rounds, and quartered
5 plum tomatoes (about ¾ pound), coarsely chopped
1 tablespoon tomato paste
1½ cups frozen peas
1 large yellow squash (about ½ pound), cut into matchsticks
¼ cup chopped parsley

1. In a stockpot or large saucepan, place the beef shanks, veal bones (if using), and water. Bring to a boil over high heat, skimming any foam that rises to the surface.

2. Add the onions, carrots, celery, salt, bay leaf, marjoram, basil, and peppercorns. Reduce the heat to low, partially cover, and simmer for at least 5 hours (the longer the broth cooks, the more concentrated the beef flavor will be).

3. Remove the beef shanks and, when they're cool enough to handle, trim the meat off the bones and cut into bite-size pieces. Cover the meat and refrigerate.

4. Strain the beef broth through a sieve lined with a double thickness of dampened cheesecloth. Discard the solids and refrigerate the broth until the fat hardens enough to be easily removed, about 6 hours. (If you are pressed for time, you can remove the fat from the broth without refrigerating it, although this is not as effective. Skim most of the clear fat from the surface with a spoon and carefully blot up as much of the remaining fat from the surface as possible with pieces of paper towel.)

5. Return the broth to a large saucepan and bring to a boil over high heat. Add the barley, reduce the heat to medium-low, and simmer until tender, about 30 minutes.

6. Add the turnips, tomatoes, and tomato paste, and simmer, partially covered, for another 30 minutes. Meanwhile, let the beef come to room temperature.

7. Add the beef, peas, yellow squash, and parsley, and continue simmering until the squash is tender, about 5 minutes longer. Serve the soup hot.   *8 servings*

Vegetable-Beef Soup with Barley

Double-Mushroom Soup

Dried mushrooms add an extra measure of earthiness to this rich and delicious soup. Any supermarket dried mushrooms will be fine, but if dried aren't available, increase the fresh mushrooms to one pound, and, in place of the mushroom soaking liquid, add another cup of chicken broth to the soup in Step 2.

1 ounce dried mushrooms, such as Polish
   mushrooms, porcini, or cèpes
1 cup hot water
5 tablespoons butter
1 cup chopped shallots (about 8 medium), or
   1 cup chopped onion

¾ pound fresh mushrooms, chopped
3 tablespoons flour
2 cups canned chicken broth
1 tablespoon dry sherry
½ cup light cream or half-and-half
⅛ teaspoon pepper

    1. In a small bowl, soak the dried mushrooms in the hot water until softened, 5 to 10 minutes. Reserving the soaking liquid, drain the mushrooms, coarsely chop, and set aside. Strain the soaking liquid through a coffee filter or paper towel and set aside.

    2. In a medium saucepan, melt the butter over medium heat. Add the shallots and sauté, stirring occasionally, until softened but not browned, about 5 minutes. Add the fresh mushrooms and cook for 3 minutes. Stir in the flour. Increase the heat to medium-high and blend in ½ cup of the chicken broth. Stir in the remaining 1½ cups chicken broth.

    3. Add the chopped dried mushrooms, the strained mushroom soaking liquid, and the sherry. Reduce the heat to medium-low, cover, and simmer for 20 minutes.

    4. Stir in the cream and pepper, and serve the soup hot.   *4 servings*

Southern Shrimp Bisque

A bisque is a creamy, rich, and smooth shellfish soup. It is often served in the South as an elegant first course for a sit-down dinner.

2 cups water
2 small white onions, whole and unpeeled
1 bay leaf
6 peppercorns
1 teaspoon salt
1 pound shrimp, in the shell
¼ cup raw rice
1 cup canned chicken broth

1 medium green bell pepper, diced (about
   1 cup)
1 medium carrot, diced (about ½ cup)
½ cup chopped shallots (about 4 medium),
   or ½ cup chopped onion
¼ cup diced celery
1 tablespoon dry sherry
½ cup heavy cream

    1. In a medium saucepan, bring the water, onions, bay leaf, peppercorns, and salt to a boil. Cover and cook for 10 minutes. Add the shrimp, reduce the heat to

medium-low, and simmer, uncovered, until the shrimp have just turned pink, 2 to 5 minutes.

2. Drain the shrimp, straining and reserving the broth. When the shrimp are cool enough to handle, shell and devein them. Mince the shrimp and set aside loosely covered.

3. In a medium saucepan, bring the reserved shrimp broth and rice to a boil. Reduce the heat to medium-low and cook, covered, until the rice is tender, about 15 minutes.

4. Increase the heat to medium-high and add the chicken broth, green pepper, carrot, shallots, celery, and sherry. Reduce the heat to medium-low, cover, and simmer for 5 minutes. Add the reserved minced shrimp and cream. Return to a simmer, uncovered, and cook to heat through, 1 to 2 minutes. Serve hot.   *4 servings*

Potato-Leek Soup

Potatoes and leeks are traditional partners in homey soups, such as this, as well as in the more sophisticated vichyssoise. This recipe calls for a mixture of boiling and baking potatoes, and for a yam, which adds a touch of color and extra flavor. For a richer soup, stir in ½ cup of heavy cream just before serving.

¼ pound bacon (4 to 6 slices)
1 pound leeks (white part only), washed and
  coarsely chopped (about 3 medium)
1 tablespoon flour
4½ cups canned chicken broth
1 medium baking potato, peeled and
  diced
1 cup peeled and diced red potato

2 cups peeled and diced white boiling potato
2 cups peeled and diced yam (about
  1 medium)
¾ to 1 teaspoon nutmeg
¼ teaspoon pepper, preferably white
2 tablespoons chopped parsley

1. In a 3- to 4-quart saucepan or soup pot, cook the bacon over medium heat until crisp, 8 to 10 minutes. Reserving the fat in the pan, drain the bacon on paper towels; crumble and set aside.

2. Add the leeks to the bacon fat and sauté over medium heat, stirring frequently, until softened but not browned, about 15 minutes.

3. Add the flour and cook, stirring, for 30 seconds. Add the broth, potatoes, and yam. Increase the heat to high and bring to a boil. Reduce the heat to medium-low, cover, and simmer until the potatoes are very tender, 20 to 30 minutes. Let the soup cool slightly.

4. In a blender or food processor, purée the soup. Return the soup to the saucepan and stir in the nutmeg and pepper. Over low heat, bring the soup to a gentle simmer.

5. Ladle the soup into individual soup bowls, sprinkle each serving with the parsley and bacon, and serve hot.   *6 servings*

ROOT VEGETABLES

The earthiest ingredients used in country cooking, root vegetables—carrots, parsnips, turnips, rutabagas, and the like—are prized more for their assertive flavors than for their appearance. While most need to be scrubbed or peeled and then enhanced with seasonings and sauces, all make welcome additions to soups and stews, and fine accompaniments to roasts.

When buying root vegetables, look for firm specimens with as few bruises and scars as possible. The smallest and youngest are usually the best, although celery root (actually a variety of celery called celeriac, with an intense celery flavor) and rutabagas are tasty regardless of size. Most root vegetables are available year round, but their prices and quality are likely to be better in the fall and winter.

Beets, carrots, and turnips are frequently sold with their greens to show freshness. Before storing these vegetables, cut off the greens; otherwise they will continue to draw moisture from the roots. Carrots and their cousins, parsnips and parsley root (which tastes like celery root with parsley overtones), keep best in the refrigerator; many other root vegetables will last for months in a cool, dark, dry, and well-ventilated place.

Root vegetables are packed with minerals and vitamins and are generally low in calories. While the majority taste best cooked, some—like turnips, celery root, and carrots—are equally delicious eaten raw.

celery root

turnips

yams

carrots

parsnips

beets

rutabagas

parsley root

potatoes

Plum Tomato Soup

To convert this recipe to a cream of tomato soup, soak eight crushed unsalted saltine crackers in a cup of heavy cream, then stir them into the soup just before serving.

1 pound fresh plum tomatoes, coarsely chopped (about 3 cups)

1 can (14 ounces) whole plum tomatoes, with their juice

½ teaspoon baking soda

1 cup canned chicken broth

1 tablespoon tomato paste

2 tablespoons chopped fresh basil, or ¾ teaspoon dried

1 teaspoon sugar

2 medium leeks (white part only), washed and finely chopped (about 2 cups), or 2 cups finely chopped onion

1. In a 2-quart nonreactive saucepan, combine the fresh and canned tomatoes with their juice, and bring to a boil over medium-high heat. Add the baking soda and cook, stirring, for 1 minute.

2. Stir in the chicken broth, tomato paste, basil, sugar, and leeks. Reduce the heat to medium-low, cover, and simmer for 1 hour. Serve the soup hot.   *4 servings*

Cheddar Cheese Soup with Cauliflower

For an interesting color contrast, garnish this all-white soup with some grated sharp yellow Cheddar cheese.

3 tablespoons butter

1 small onion, chopped (about ½ cup)

2 cloves garlic, minced

3 cups finely chopped cauliflower florets (about 1 small head)

¾ cup diced green bell pepper (about ½ large)

1 medium carrot, finely chopped (about ½ cup)

3 tablespoons flour

3 cups canned chicken broth

2 teaspoons Dijon mustard

2 cups grated sharp white Cheddar cheese (about ½ pound)

¼ cup chopped parsley

1. In a 2- to 3-quart saucepan, melt the butter over medium heat. Add the onion and garlic, and sauté until softened but not browned, about 10 minutes.

2. Add the cauliflower, green pepper, and carrot. Increase the heat to medium-high and sauté, stirring frequently, until the vegetables are crisp-tender, about 5 minutes. Increase the heat to high, add the flour, and cook, stirring, for 1 minute.

3. Gradually pour in the chicken broth and whisk until slightly thickened. Blend in the mustard. Reduce the heat to low and simmer the soup, partially covered, for 15 minutes, stirring occasionally.

4. A handful at a time, add the grated cheese and stir until it is completely melted. Increase the heat to medium-high and bring almost to a boil. Sprinkle the soup with the parsley and serve hot.   *4 to 6 servings*

Plum Tomato Soup

Yellow Split Pea, Yam, and Carrot Soup (left)
and Fresh Pea Soup (right)

Yellow Split Pea, Yam, and Carrot Soup

In this warming winter soup, the rich color of yellow split peas is enhanced by the addition of a yam and carrots.

1 small smoked ham hock (about 1 pound)
4 cups water
1¼ cups yellow split peas (about ½ pound),
   rinsed and picked over
2 medium carrots, diced (about 1 cup)
1 small yam, peeled and cut into chunks

5 medium scallions (white part only), chopped
   (about ⅓ cup)
1 small red bell pepper, diced (about ½ cup)
1 clove garlic, crushed through a press
½ bay leaf
Salt and pepper

1. In a 2-quart saucepan, bring the ham hock and water to a boil over medium-high heat. Boil for 4 minutes, skimming any foam that rises to the surface.

2. Add the split peas, carrots, yam, scallions, red pepper, garlic, and bay leaf, and return to a boil. Reduce the heat to medium-low, cover, and simmer until the peas are tender, 2 to 2½ hours. Discard the bay leaf.

3. Trim the meat off the ham hock and cut into bite-size pieces. With a wooden spoon, mash the vegetables lightly against the sides of the pan to make the soup smoother. Return the meat to the soup and reheat briefly, if necessary. Season the soup to taste with salt and pepper, and serve hot. *4 servings*

Fresh Pea Soup

In the summer, take advantage of the sweet, delicate flavor of peas fresh from the garden. In the winter, frozen peas are a satisfying alternative.

2 tablespoons butter
1 cup finely chopped shallots (about 11
  medium), or 1 small onion, finely chopped
2 tablespoons flour
3 cups canned chicken broth

2 pounds fresh peas, shelled, or 2 cups frozen
  peas, thawed
4 cups torn Boston lettuce leaves (about
  1 head)
Salt and pepper

    1. In a medium saucepan, melt the butter over medium heat. Add the shallots and sauté until softened but not browned, 3 to 4 minutes. Sprinkle in the flour and stir to blend.

    2. Stir in the broth, increase the heat to medium-high, and bring to a boil. Add the peas and lettuce; reduce the heat to medium-low, cover, and simmer until the peas are tender, about 15 minutes for fresh and 5 minutes for frozen.

    3. Let the soup cool slightly. Then, in a food processor or blender, purée the soup. Return the puréed soup to a clean saucepan and bring to a boil over medium heat.

    4. Season the soup to taste with salt and pepper, and serve hot.　　　*4 servings*

COUNTRY TUREENS

Soups and stews have traditionally been considered simple fare, but when they are served in pretty tureens, they can turn meals into festive occasions.

The contemporary tureens at right are but a few of the many styles that can inspire an idea for a meal or enhance a country table. Individual melon tureens, for example, are perfect for serving chilled cantaloupe soup, while those shaped like small heads of lettuce make charming containers for fresh pea soup. To ward off winter's chill, offer hot clam chowder from a handsome fish tureen or ladle squash bisque from an acorn-shaped tureen.

Tureens also make attractive centerpieces. A pumpkin-shaped tureen filled with fruit or flowers is an ideal table decoration for a Halloween party, and a rabbit tureen overflowing with chocolate eggs is bound to delight the family at Easter.

Among the tureens in the collection at right are individual lettuce and pumpkin tureens that come in both small and large sizes. The ironstone tureen at far left on the bottom shelf is a reproduction of a c. 1820 English Staffordshire design. The earthenware tureen at far right on the same shelf bears a pattern in use since the early 1800s: Roman ruins surrounded by an oriental border. For more information on all of these tureens, see page 170.

Virginia Peanut Soup

Peanut soup is served in many parts of the Southeast (where West African cooks first introduced the legume they called a groundnut), but it has become a prized regional specialty in Virginia, one of the country's leading peanut-producing states.

2 tablespoons butter

1 medium onion, chopped (about 1¼ cups)

2 cloves garlic, minced

1 cup whole roasted unsalted peanuts plus ⅓
    cup chopped roasted unsalted peanuts

⅔ cup creamy peanut butter

3 cups canned chicken broth

½ cup light cream or half-and-half

⅛ teaspoon pepper, preferably white

2 tablespoons chopped chives

1. In a medium skillet, melt the butter over medium-high heat. Add the onion and garlic, and sauté, stirring frequently, until the onion is softened but not browned, about 10 minutes.

2. Place the sautéed onion and garlic in a blender or food processor with the 1 cup whole peanuts, and process until the mixture is the consistency of coarse peanut butter, about 1 minute. Add the creamy peanut butter and process to blend, about 30 seconds. With the machine on, gradually add ½ cup of the chicken broth and process until smooth. With the machine still running, add the remaining 2½ cups broth and the cream, and blend.

3. Transfer the soup to a medium saucepan and bring to a gentle simmer over medium heat. Stir in the pepper.

4. Ladle the soup into individual soup bowls, sprinkle each serving with the chopped peanuts and chives, and serve hot.

4 servings

Black Bean Soup

The dark, full flavor of black beans has made them a popular soup ingredient in many parts of the United States. This variation, which combines a number of regional influences, borrows its lime and sour cream garnish from Latin America.

2 cups dried black or turtle beans (about ¾
    pound), rinsed and picked over

2 ounces salt pork, diced (about ⅔ cup)

1 tablespoon vegetable oil

1 Spanish onion, chopped (about 2 cups)

3 cloves garlic, minced

3 cups canned beef broth

3 cups water

¼ cup sherry

1 can (14 ounces) whole plum tomatoes, with
    their juice

3 medium carrots, diced (about 1½ cups)

2 stalks celery, diced (about 1 cup)

1 bay leaf

1 lime, sliced into thin rounds, for garnish

About 1½ cups sour cream, for garnish

1. Place the beans in a large saucepan with water to cover by 2 inches. Bring to a boil and boil for 2 minutes. Remove from the heat, cover, and let stand for 1 hour.

2. Meanwhile, in a small saucepan of boiling water, blanch the salt pork for 5 minutes. Drain well and pat dry.

3. In a soup pot or large saucepan, heat the oil over medium-high heat. Add the salt pork, onion, and garlic, and sauté, stirring frequently, until the onion has softened but not browned, about 10 minutes.

4. Drain the beans and add them to the soup pot along with the beef broth, water, sherry, tomatoes with their juice, carrots, celery, and bay leaf. Bring to a boil, reduce the heat to medium-low, and cook, stirring occasionally, until the beans are tender, 1½ to 2 hours.

5. Discard the bay leaf. With a slotted spoon, remove the beans and place in a blender or food processor. Add about a cup of the soup liquid and process until the beans are smooth. (For a smoother, more evenly colored soup, force the bean purée through a sieve.) Stir the puréed beans back into the soup.

6. Reheat the soup over medium heat until hot. Ladle the soup into individual soup bowls. Top each serving with one or two lime slices and a generous tablespoon of sour cream.

6 servings

Turkey Chowder

Originally chowders were made only with seafood. But this style of thick, potatoey, almost stewlike soup has often been adapted for other ingredients. One of the more common adaptations is turkey chowder, undoubtedly a result of the continual search for ways to use Thanksgiving leftovers.

2 ounces salt pork, diced (about ⅔ cup)
4 tablespoons butter
3 small white onions (about ¼ pound), sliced
½ cup flour
4 cups canned chicken broth
1 pound small red potatoes, unpeeled and
  quartered

½ teaspoon thyme
3 cups cubed cooked turkey (about ¾ pound)
1 medium red bell pepper, diced (about
  1 cup)
1 cup frozen peas
1½ cups milk
¼ cup chopped parsley

1. In a small saucepan of boiling water, blanch the salt pork for 5 minutes. Drain well and pat dry.

2. In a soup pot or large saucepan, melt the butter over medium-high heat. Add the salt pork and onions, and sauté, stirring frequently, for 10 minutes.

3. Add the flour and cook, stirring, until the flour is lightly browned, about 1 minute. Gradually stir in the broth, increase the heat to high, and bring to a boil. Add the potatoes and thyme, reduce the heat to medium-low, cover, and simmer until the potatoes are tender, about 15 minutes.

4. Add the turkey, red pepper, peas, and milk, and cook for another 5 minutes to heat through. Ladle the chowder into individual bowls, sprinkle each serving with the parsley, and serve hot.

6 to 8 servings

Albóndigas Soup

In this soup from New Mexico, jalapeño-spiked meatballs (*albóndigas*) are cooked in a rich beef broth. This version is fairly light and delicate; for a heartier soup, add some cubed potatoes and cook them with the meatballs.

1 tablespoon vegetable oil
1 medium onion, chopped (about 1¼ cups)
1 clove garlic, minced
4 cups canned beef broth
1 can (14 ounces) whole plum tomatoes, with their juice
1½ teaspoons ground coriander
1 to 2 teaspoons seeded, minced fresh jalapeño pepper (see Note, page 43)

½ teaspoon black pepper
½ pound ground beef
½ pound ground pork
¼ cup raw rice
1 egg, lightly beaten
½ teaspoon salt
½ cup chopped scallion greens (2 to 3 scallions)

1. In a 3- to 4-quart soup pot or saucepan, heat the oil over medium-high heat. Add the onion and garlic, and sauté, stirring frequently, until the onion is golden, 5 to 7 minutes.

2. Add the beef broth, tomatoes with their juice, 1 teaspoon of the coriander, ½ to 1 teaspoon of the jalapeño pepper, and ¼ teaspoon of the black pepper. Increase the heat to high and bring to a boil. Reduce the heat to low and simmer, partially covered, for 20 minutes.

3. Meanwhile, in a large bowl, combine the beef, pork, rice, egg, salt, the remaining ½ teaspoon coriander, ½ to 1 teaspoon jalapeño pepper, and ¼ teaspoon black pepper. Knead the ingredients together with your hands and then beat with a wooden spoon until the meatball mixture is light and fluffy. Shape the meatballs by scooping up tablespoons of the mixture and rolling them into balls.

4. Drop the meatballs into the simmering soup and stir gently to separate them. Partially cover and simmer the soup for another 30 minutes, stirring occasionally.

5. Sprinkle the soup with the scallion greens and serve hot.   *4 servings*

Butternut-Apple Soup

This comforting and flavorful soup can be made with any orange-fleshed winter squash, such as Hubbard or acorn. You can also use canned pumpkin: substitute one can (16 ounces) unsweetened solid-pack purée for the squash.

*B*utternut squash, as well as Hubbard and acorn squash, are known as winter squash. Widely available in the fall and winter months, these squash are distinguished by their hard shells, which keep them fresh for long periods of time. When buying any winter squash, make sure the shell is indeed hard, smooth, and unblemished.

1 medium butternut squash (about 2 pounds)	*2 teaspoons maple syrup or brown sugar*
2 tablespoons butter	*½ cup heavy cream*
1 medium onion, chopped (about 1¼ cups)	*1 red-skinned apple, thinly sliced,*
1 cup unsweetened applesauce	*for garnish*
1½ cups canned chicken broth	*Cinnamon, for garnish*

1. Preheat the oven to 375°. Line a baking sheet with aluminum foil.
2. Cut the squash in half lengthwise. Place the squash halves cut-side down on the baking sheet and bake for 25 to 30 minutes, or until the thickest part is tender when pierced with a knife.
3. Remove the squash seeds and strings, and scoop the flesh out of the shell. With a wooden spoon or potato masher, mash the squash to a coarse purée.
4. In a medium saucepan, melt the butter over medium heat. Add the onion and cook, stirring frequently, until softened but not browned, about 10 minutes.
5. Stir in the squash purée, the applesauce, chicken broth, and maple syrup. Reduce the heat to medium-low, cover, and simmer the soup for 15 minutes.
6. Remove the pan from the heat and stir in the cream. Ladle the soup into individual bowls and garnish each serving with several thin slices of apple arranged in a fan shape; dust with cinnamon.

4 servings

Chicken-Corn Soup with Noodles

For this Lancaster County favorite, Pennsylvania-German cooks traditionally make their own noodles (called rivels) by crumbling egg pasta dough into the simmering broth to form small pasta dumplings.

3½-pound chicken, rinsed and quartered	*2 teaspoons salt*
8 cups water	*2 cups medium-wide egg noodles*
2 medium carrots, whole and unpeeled	*2 cups corn kernels, fresh (about 4 large ears),*
1 medium leek, washed but left whole	*or frozen, thawed*
½ cup (packed) celery leaves	*1 small red bell pepper, cut into matchsticks*
10 sprigs of parsley	*(about ¾ cup)*
2 cloves garlic, lightly crushed	*Pinch of saffron*
5 peppercorns	*¼ cup chopped fresh dill*

1. In a stockpot or large saucepan, bring the chicken and water to a boil over high heat, skimming any foam that rises to the surface. Add the carrots, leek, celery leaves,

Chicken-Corn Soup with Noodles

parsley, garlic, peppercorns, and salt. Reduce the heat to low and simmer, partially covered, for 30 minutes.

2. Remove the chicken from the broth. When it's cool enough to handle, skin and bone it (reserve the bones), and cut the meat into bite-size pieces. Cover and refrigerate. Return the bones to the broth and simmer, partially covered, for 1 hour.

3. Strain the broth. Discard the solids and refrigerate the broth until the fat hardens enough to be easily removed, about 6 hours.

4. Return the broth to a large saucepan and bring to a boil over high heat. Add the noodles, corn, red pepper, reserved chicken, and saffron to the broth. Reduce the heat to medium and cook until the noodles are tender but still firm, about 5 minutes.

5. Stir in the dill and serve the soup hot.   *8 servings*

Meat, Poultry, and Seafood

main dishes for all occasions

Yankee Pot Roast … Chicken Pot Pie … New England Boiled Dinner … Red Flannel Hash. No book on country cooking would be complete without recipes for these and other traditional main-course dishes, popular since colonial times. Yet many of the recipes we take for granted were the invention of frugal necessity. Because beef was in limited supply in the colonies, New Englanders made pot roasts and boiled dinners to utilize tough cuts of meat. And while chickens were more common, they were hardly the plump specimens we know today; in fact, chicken pot pies were a popular way of disguising the scrawnier birds. Turkeys, which had to be hunted, were a luxury for the early settlers. Then, as now, they were eaten mainly at Thanksgiving and Christmas.

Many of the recipes on the following pages are a reminder of the ingenuity that was required to survive in those early days; others are the product of later and more affluent tastes. Whether you prefer meat, poultry, or seafood, this chapter offers suggestions for a wide variety of country meals.

Ready for the table: Yankee Pot Roast with potatoes, turnips, and carrots.

Chicken Pot Pie in a Cheese Crust

Pot pie is an American dish that has been around since the 18th century. If you've tasted only the frozen commercial variety, you haven't had a real pot pie.

PASTRY
1½ cups flour
¼ cup grated Parmesan cheese (about 1 ounce)
2 tablespoons minced parsley
½ teaspoon salt
¼ teaspoon pepper
1 stick (4 ounces) chilled butter, cut into
  tablespoons
3 to 4 tablespoons ice water

FILLING
2 cups canned chicken broth

¼ pound small white onions, quartered
2 cups peeled, diced yam or sweet potato
¾ to 1 teaspoon crumbled sage
¼ teaspoon pepper
2 medium carrots, cut into ¼-inch rounds
2 cups broccoli florets
½ cup diced celery
¼ cup flour
4 tablespoons butter, softened to room
  temperature
3 cups cooked chicken, in bite-size pieces
1 egg, beaten

1. Make the pastry: In a large bowl, combine the flour, Parmesan, parsley, salt, and pepper. Cut the butter in until the mixture resembles coarse meal. Sprinkle on 3 tablespoons of ice water and work it into the dough, adding up to 1 more tablespoon of water to form a dough that can be gathered into a ball. Divide the dough in half, press each portion into a disc shape, wrap in plastic wrap, and refrigerate for at least 30 minutes.

2. Make the filling: In a large saucepan, bring the chicken broth to a boil over medium-high heat. Add the onions, yam, sage, and pepper, and cook until the yam is just tender, about 5 minutes. Add the carrots, broccoli, and celery, and cook until the carrots and broccoli are just tender, about 5 minutes longer.

3. In a small bowl, with your fingertips, thoroughly blend the flour with the butter. Increase the heat under the saucepan to high, pinch off pieces of the flour-butter mixture, and drop them one at a time into the pan, stirring to incorporate after each addition. Cook until the sauce has thickened slightly, 2 to 3 minutes. Remove the pan from the heat and stir in the chicken.

4. Preheat the oven to 425°.

5. Roll one half of the dough into a 12-inch circle and fit it into a 9-inch pie pan, letting the extra dough hang over the edges. Spoon the filling into the pastry shell.

6. Roll the other half of the dough into a 9-inch circle and place it on top of the filling. Trim the overhang to an even ½ inch all the way around. Fold the overhang in over the top crust, crimping to seal. Cut steam vents in the top crust and brush with the beaten egg.

7. Bake the pie for 15 minutes. Lower the oven temperature to 325° and bake 10 to 15 minutes longer, or until the crust is golden. Serve hot.   *6 to 8 servings*

Chicken Pot Pie in a Cheese Crust

All-American Fish Dinner

All-American Fish Dinner

In most regions that have access to freshly caught fish or shellfish, cooks have developed some version of a simple boiled seafood dinner. Fish and/or shellfish, vegetables, and sometimes spices and smoked meat are cooked in a huge pot of boiling water, then served with melted butter or a spicy tomato sauce. This all-American recipe pays homage to both coasts by calling for salmon and scrod, and to the South by including hot sausage.

½ pound Italian hot sausage,
* casings removed*
1 medium onion, coarsely chopped
* (about 1¼ cups)*
2 cloves garlic, minced
4 cups water
2 cups canned chicken broth
12 small white onions, peeled and left whole
9 small red potatoes, unpeeled and quartered

4 ears of corn, cut into 1-inch sections
1 pound boneless salmon, cut into 2-inch
* chunks*
1 pound boneless scrod, cut into 2-inch
* chunks*
½ pound medium shrimp (see Note)
1 cup chopped scallions (about 5 medium)
Melted butter
Salt and pepper

1. In a large soup pot or stockpot, sauté the sausage over medium heat for 5 minutes, breaking up the meat with a spoon as it cooks. Add the chopped onion and the garlic, and cook for 5 minutes longer.

2. Add the water, broth, whole white onions, potatoes, and corn. Increase the heat to high and bring to a boil. Reduce the heat to medium-low, cover, and simmer until the onions and potatoes are tender, 10 to 15 minutes.

3. Increase the heat to medium-high. Add the salmon, scrod, and shrimp. Reduce the heat to medium-low, cover, and simmer, stirring gently, until the seafood is opaque and cooked through, about 5 minutes.

4. Just before serving, stir in the scallions. Remove the fish and vegetables with a slotted spoon and serve with melted butter, salt, and pepper. If desired, serve the broth separately.   *8 to 10 servings*

NOTE: The shrimp can be shelled if desired, but cooking them in their shells adds flavor to the broth.

Pan-Fried Trout with Mint and Bacon

These trout taste best cooked over an open fire. If fresh mint isn't available, tuck a few sprigs of parsley into the fish and serve with parsley butter.

4 whole trout (about 1 pound each), cleaned,	*¼ cup flour*
with head and tail intact	*½ teaspoon salt*
1 stick (4 ounces) plus 2 tablespoons butter	*¼ teaspoon pepper*
1 cup finely chopped mint	*¼ pound bacon (4 to 6 slices)*
¼ cup yellow cornmeal	*Juice of 1 lemon plus lemon wedges*

1. Preheat the oven to 200°. Wash the trout well and pat dry inside and out.

2. In a small saucepan, melt the butter over low heat. In a small bowl, moisten ½ cup of the mint with about 2 tablespoons of the melted butter. Spread this mint in the cavity of each fish. Add the remaining ½ cup mint to the butter remaining in the saucepan. Set the mint butter aside and keep warm.

3. In a shallow bowl, combine the cornmeal, flour, salt, and pepper. Thoroughly dredge each fish in the seasoned cornmeal and set aside.

4. In a large skillet (see Note), cook the bacon over medium heat until crisp, about 10 minutes. Reserving the fat in the pan, drain the bacon on paper towels; crumble and set aside.

5. Heat the bacon fat over medium heat, add 2 of the trout to the skillet, and fry until well browned, about 4 minutes on each side. The fish should be opaque at its thickest point. Remove the fish to a platter and keep warm in the oven while you repeat with the remaining trout.

6. Add the lemon juice to the skillet and bring to a boil over high heat. Stir in the crumbled bacon and spoon over the trout. Serve the trout with warm mint butter and lemon wedges.   *4 servings*

NOTE: If you have two large skillets, you can cook the fish all at once. Divide the bacon fat between the two skillets in Step 4 and use only one of the skillets in Step 6.

To calculate the proper cooking time for whole fish or fish fillets, try the Canadian Department of Fisheries method: Measure the fish at its thickest point, then cook the fish ten minutes for every inch of thickness, regardless of cooking technique. To double-check for doneness, press the fish with your finger; if it springs back, it is done.

Country Meat Loaf with Carrots

A layer of carrot halves baked in the middle of this old-fashioned meat loaf gives it a colorful mosaic look when sliced.

2 large carrots, halved lengthwise
1 pound ground beef
½ pound pork sausage, casings removed
1 medium onion, chopped (about 1¼ cups)
¾ cup old-fashioned rolled oats
½ cup ketchup

1 egg, lightly beaten
1 tablespoon Worcestershire sauce
1 teaspoon salt
¼ teaspoon pepper
4 slices bacon (about ¼ pound)
1 tablespoon chopped parsley, for garnish

    1. Preheat the oven to 375°
    2. In a medium saucepan of boiling water, blanch the carrots until just tender, 5 to 10 minutes. Set aside.
    3. In a large bowl, combine the beef and sausage with the onion, oats, ketchup, egg, Worcestershire sauce, salt, and pepper.
    4. Spread half the meat loaf mixture in a 4 x 8-inch loaf pan. Place the carrot halves lengthwise in a single layer on top of the meat. Cover with the remaining meat loaf mixture and pack down. Place the bacon strips side by side down the length of the meat loaf.
    5. Bake the meat loaf for 30 minutes. Turn the bacon strips over and bake for 30 minutes longer.
    6. Slice the meat loaf and serve hot, sprinkled with the parsley.   *4 to 6 servings*

Yankee Pot Roast

Frugal New Englanders are credited with this method of tenderizing tough cuts of beef by "roasting" them in a deep pot filled with broth and vegetables. Other inexpensive cuts such as brisket, round, or rump can be substituted for the chuck roast.

½ cup flour
1 teaspoon salt
½ teaspoon pepper
4-pound chuck roast
¼ cup bacon drippings (rendered from
    about ¼ pound bacon)
1 tablespoon vegetable oil
2 cups canned beef broth
2 cups water

2 cloves garlic, crushed through a press
1 teaspoon thyme
1 bay leaf
6 small boiling potatoes (about 1¼ pounds),
    peeled and quartered
2 to 3 medium white turnips (about 1¼
    pounds), peeled and quartered
4 medium carrots, cut into 2-inch lengths
¼ cup chopped parsley

    1. In a small bowl, combine the flour, salt, and pepper. Coat the roast with the seasoned flour, tapping off any excess. Reserve the remaining dredging flour.

2. In a Dutch oven or flameproof casserole, heat the bacon drippings and the oil over medium heat. Add the roast and brown slowly, turning to color all sides, about 30 minutes. Add more oil if necessary to prevent sticking.

3. Add the beef broth, water, garlic, thyme, and bay leaf. Reduce the heat to low, cover, and simmer for 2 hours, turning the roast occasionally.

4. Add the potatoes, turnips, and carrots, and simmer, covered, until the meat and vegetables are tender, about 30 minutes longer.

5. Remove the meat and vegetables from the Dutch oven; place on a platter and cover loosely with foil to keep warm. Discard the bay leaf.

6. Slowly whisk 1 cup of the pot roast liquid into the reserved dredging flour. Place the Dutch oven over medium-high heat and whisk in the flour mixture. Bring the gravy to a boil and boil until thickened, 2 to 3 minutes. Stir in the parsley.

7. Slice the pot roast and serve with the vegetables and gravy. *8 servings*

New England Boiled Dinner

If you have any leftovers from this simple American classic, use them—in true Yankee tradition—to make either a corned beef hash or Red Flannel Hash (page 48).

4 pounds corned beef
1 bay leaf
8 peppercorns
1 clove garlic
1 stalk celery, halved
5 medium carrots, 2 cut in half and 3 cut into 2-inch lengths

5 medium boiling potatoes, peeled and quartered
2 small white turnips, peeled and quartered
2 small onions, cut into wedges
½ medium head cabbage, cut into 8 wedges
2 small beets, peeled and quartered
¼ cup chopped parsley

1. Place the corned beef in a large soup pot or stockpot, with enough water to cover completely. Bring to a boil over high heat.

2. As soon as the water boils, pour it off and add fresh water to cover the corned beef. Add the bay leaf, peppercorns, garlic, celery, and the halved carrots. Bring the water back to a boil over high heat, skimming any foam that rises to the surface. Reduce the heat to medium-low, cover, and simmer, skimming as necessary, until the meat is tender but still firm, about 2½ hours.

3. About 30 minutes before the meat is done, remove and discard the bay leaf, peppercorns, garlic, and broth vegetables. Add the 2-inch carrot pieces, potatoes, turnips, and onions. After 15 minutes, add the cabbage.

4. At the same time you add the carrots to the meat, in a medium saucepan, bring 3 cups of water to a boil. Add the beets, reduce the heat to medium-low, cover, and cook until tender, 25 to 30 minutes. Drain.

5. When the meat and vegetables are cooked, drain and cut the meat into slices. Arrange the meat on a platter and surround it with vegetables (including the beets). Sprinkle with the parsley and serve. *6 servings*

Country Captain

There seems to be some dispute as to the origins of this Southern curried chicken dish. Residents of Georgia claim that the dish, along with curry spices, made its way to this country via the spice trade and the seaport city of Savannah. Eliza Leslie, author of *Miss Leslie's New Cookery Book*, published in 1857, claimed that its route to the American South was more circuitous, giving credit to a British colonial army officer who brought the recipe back to England from India. Whatever its source, the method of currying chicken was enthusiastically adopted by Southern cooks, particularly in coastal regions where exotic spices were readily available. In fact, early cookbooks even include recipes for homemade curry powder, such as this one from Mrs. Mary Randolph's *Virginia Housewife* (1831): "One Ounce Turmeric, one [dozen] Coriander Seed, one [dozen] Cummin Seed, one [dozen] white Ginger, one of Nutmeg, one of Mace, and one of Cayenne Pepper; pound it all together, and pass them through a fine Sieve; bottle and cork it well—one Teaspoonful is sufficient to season any made Dish."

Although curry powder can be a blend of as many as a hundred spices, most Indian curries contain six basic seasonings: coriander, cumin, and fenugreek for fragrance and flavor; turmeric for a rich golden color; and cayenne and black pepper for spiciness.

½ cup flour
1 teaspoon salt
¼ teaspoon pepper
2½-pound chicken, cut into 8 serving pieces, rinsed and patted dry
2 tablespoons butter
2 tablespoons vegetable oil
1 medium onion, chopped (about 1¼ cups)
2 to 3 cloves garlic, lightly crushed

2 tablespoons curry powder
½ teaspoon thyme
2 cans (14 ounces each) whole tomatoes, with their juice
1 cup raisins
¼ cup chopped parsley
½ cup sliced almonds, toasted (see Note)
Steamed rice

1. In a shallow bowl, mix together the flour, ½ teaspoon of the salt, and the pepper. Dredge the chicken in the seasoned flour.

2. In a large skillet, melt the butter in the oil over medium-high heat until very hot. Add the chicken and brown well on all sides, 15 to 20 minutes.

3. Remove the chicken and set aside. Pour off all but 1 tablespoon of the fat from the skillet. Add the onion, garlic, curry powder, thyme, and the remaining ½ teaspoon salt to the skillet. Cook over low heat for 5 minutes, stirring to loosen the browned bits clinging to the pan.

4. Add the tomatoes with their juice, breaking them up with a spoon. Return the chicken, skin-side up, to the skillet, cover, and simmer until the chicken is tender when pierced with a fork, 20 to 30 minutes.

5. Stir in the raisins and chopped parsley. Sprinkle the chicken with the toasted almonds and serve hot over steamed rice.   *4 to 6 servings*

NOTE: To toast the almonds, place them on an ungreased cookie sheet in a preheated 375° oven for 10 minutes, or until golden.

Country Captain

Stuffed Roast Turkey

As an alternative to this whole wheat-mushroom dressing, try one of the stuffing recipes on the following page. If there is any extra stuffing, place it in a greased baking pan, cover the pan with aluminum foil, and bake it in the oven for the last 20 to 30 minutes of the turkey's roasting time.

STUFFING
1 stick (4 ounces) butter
1 cup chopped scallions (about 5 medium)
1 cup diced carrots (about 2 medium)
2 to 3 cloves garlic, minced
1 pound mushrooms, finely chopped
10 slices stale firm-textured whole-wheat bread,
   cubed (about 6 cups)
¼ cup chopped parsley

1 teaspoon thyme
1 teaspoon salt
½ teaspoon pepper

TURKEY
12-pound turkey, well rinsed (see Note)
1 stick (4 ounces) butter
2 teaspoons salt
1 teaspoon pepper

1. Preheat the oven to 425°.

2. Make the stuffing: In a large skillet, melt 2 tablespoons of the butter over medium heat. Add the scallions, carrots, and garlic, and sauté until the scallions are softened but not browned, about 5 minutes. Increase the heat to medium-high, add the remaining 6 tablespoons butter and the mushrooms, and sauté until the mushrooms are softened but not browned, 5 to 10 minutes.

3. Meanwhile, in a large bowl, combine the bread cubes, parsley, thyme, salt, and pepper. Stir in the sautéed vegetables. Cool the stuffing slightly before using.

4. Prepare the turkey: Stuff the turkey loosely and truss. Blend 6 tablespoons of the butter with the salt and pepper, and rub the outside of the turkey with the seasoned butter. Place the turkey, breast-side up, in a roasting pan and roast until golden brown, 30 to 35 minutes. In a small saucepan, melt the remaining 2 tablespoons butter.

5. Turn the turkey on its side, baste with the pan juices, and brush with 1 tablespoon of the melted butter. Lower the oven temperature to 350° and roast for 45 minutes, basting after about 20 minutes.

6. Turn the turkey onto its other side, baste with the pan juices, and brush with the remaining 1 tablespoon melted butter. Roast for another 45 minutes, basting after about 20 minutes. Should any portion of the turkey seem to be browning too quickly, cover it loosely with aluminum foil.

7. If the turkey is not done (it should measure 180° on an instant-reading meat thermometer inserted into the thickest part of the leg), roast it, breast-side up, for another 20 minutes, continuing to baste, and check again. Remove the turkey to a carving board and let rest at least 15 minutes before carving. *6 to 8 servings*

NOTE: If you are planning to stuff the turkey with the Wild Rice-Sweet Pepper Stuffing (page 42), reserve the giblets.

Stuffed Roast Turkey with Wild Rice-Sweet Pepper Stuffing

Sausage-Apple Stuffing

Using an unpeeled apple not only makes this stuffing recipe easier to prepare, but also adds a touch of color.

1 pound pork sausage, casings removed
2 tablespoons butter
4 stalks celery, chopped (about 2 cups)
1 large red-skinned apple, unpeeled and cubed
 (about 2 cups)
1 medium onion, chopped (about 1¼ cups)
1 clove garlic, minced
½ cup canned chicken broth

16 slices stale firm-textured white bread, cut
 into cubes (about 10 cups)
1 cup raisins
¼ cup chopped parsley
1 teaspoon crumbled sage
½ teaspoon salt
½ teaspoon pepper

    1. In a large skillet, cook the sausage over medium heat for 10 minutes, breaking it up with a wooden spoon.

    2. Add the butter, celery, apple, onion, garlic, and broth, and cook for 10 minutes longer.

    3. Add the bread, raisins, parsley, sage, salt, and pepper to the skillet, and stir to combine. Cool the stuffing slightly before using.　　　　*Makes about 9 cups*

Wild Rice-Sweet Pepper Stuffing

The nuttiness of the wild rice and the sweet crunch of the bell peppers combine to make an unusual stuffing for roast turkey; be sure to set aside the turkey giblets for use in this recipe. If you cannot find yellow bell peppers in your supermarket or farmer's market, use a second red pepper.

2 cups raw wild rice
Turkey giblets
1½ cups canned chicken broth
1 cup water
½ teaspoon salt
½ teaspoon black pepper
1 stick (4 ounces) butter
4 cups chopped leeks, or 4 cups chopped onion

1 large green bell pepper, diced (about 1½
 cups)
1 large red bell pepper, diced (about 1½ cups)
1 large yellow or orange bell pepper, diced
 (about 1½ cups)
2 cloves garlic, minced
2 tablespoons dry sherry
2 teaspoons marjoram

    1. Cook the wild rice according to the package directions and drain well.

    2. Meanwhile, in a medium saucepan, bring the giblets, chicken broth, water, salt, and pepper to a boil over medium-high heat. Reduce the heat to medium-low, cover, and simmer until the gizzard is tender, about 30 minutes.

    3. Drain the giblets, reserving the broth. When cool enough to handle, chop the giblets and set aside, loosely covered.

4. In a large skillet, melt the butter over medium heat. Add the leeks, bell peppers, and garlic, and sauté, stirring frequently, until the vegetables are softened but not browned, about 10 minutes. Stir in the reserved broth, sherry, and marjoram. In a large bowl, combine the vegetables, giblets, and wild rice. Let the stuffing cool slightly before using.

Makes about 10 cups

Chicken with Sauce Piquant

Sauce piquant (which loosely translates as hot sauce) is a spicy tomato-based sauce that is a staple of Cajun cuisine. South Louisianans serve sauce piquant over just about anything—including rabbit, turtle, alligator, and squirrel—and celebrate its versatility in an annual Sauce Piquant Festival in Raceland, Louisiana.

1 cup flour
3 large cloves garlic, minced
½ teaspoon pepper, preferably white
¼ teaspoon cayenne pepper
1½ teaspoons thyme
1½ teaspoons salt
2½ pounds chicken parts, rinsed
  and patted dry
About 4 cups peanut oil, for frying
2 medium onions, chopped
  (about 2½ cups)

2 medium red bell peppers, chopped
  (about 2 cups)
2 stalks celery, chopped (about 1 cup)
1 cup chopped leeks, or 1 cup chopped onion
1 can (14 ounces) whole tomatoes,
  with their juice
1 can (15 ounces) tomato purée
1½ cups canned chicken broth
1 fresh jalapeño pepper, seeded
  and minced (see Note)
Steamed rice

1. In a shallow bowl, mix together the flour, garlic, white pepper, cayenne, 1 teaspoon of the thyme, and 1 teaspoon of the salt. Dredge the chicken in the seasoned flour; reserve the remaining dredging flour and set aside.

2. In a large skillet, heat ½ inch of the oil to 350° over medium-high heat. Add the chicken, skin-side down, in batches if necessary, and fry until browned and crisp, 5 to 8 minutes on each side. Drain the chicken on paper towels.

3. Carefully pour the oil into a heatproof container. Return 2 tablespoons of the oil to the skillet. Add the reserved dredging flour, and cook over high heat, stirring constantly, until the flour is golden brown, 30 seconds to 1 minute. Add the onions, red peppers, celery, leeks, tomatoes with their juice, tomato purée, chicken broth, jalapeño pepper, and remaining ½ teaspoon thyme and ½ teaspoon salt. Cook the sauce for about 5 minutes, stirring occasionally.

4. Simmer over medium-low heat, partially covered, for 30 minutes.

5. Return the chicken to the skillet and simmer until heated through, 15 to 25 minutes. Serve the chicken and sauce hot over steamed rice.   *8 servings*

NOTE: After handling jalapeños, do not touch your face or eyes until you have washed your hands well with hot soapy water.

Fourth of July Salmon with Egg Sauce

For many New Englanders, Fourth of July celebrations would not be the same without the traditional meal of poached salmon with egg sauce, new potatoes, baby peas, and strawberry shortcake. By happy coincidence, Atlantic salmon begin to run at the same time that gardens in the Northeast are yielding their first produce.

In the 1927 cookbook
Breakfasts, Luncheons,
and Dinners, *published by*
the Boston Cooking School,
Lime Gingerade is recommended
as the ideal beverage for a
Fourth of July lawn party: Add
"to each quart of orange pekoe
tea an equal volume of ginger
ale and the juice of two green
limes. Sweeten to taste....
Pour over a block of ice
in a punch bowl, and serve
garnished with crystallized
fruit or cubes of
amber jelly."

1 small onion, halved
5 peppercorns
1 bay leaf
4 whole sprigs dill, plus additional sprigs,
   for garnish

4 salmon steaks, cut 1 inch thick (about 1½
   pounds total)
Egg Sauce (recipe follows)

1. In a large skillet, bring 3 cups of water to a boil over medium-high heat. Add the onion, peppercorns, bay leaf, and 4 sprigs of the dill. Add the salmon steaks in a single layer, making sure they are covered by liquid (add more water if necessary). Return the liquid to a simmer over medium-high heat; reduce the heat to medium-low, cover, and simmer the fish until the salmon is opaque throughout, 8 to 10 minutes. With a slotted spatula, remove the fish to a platter and cover loosely with foil to keep warm. Reserve the poaching liquid for the Egg Sauce.

2. Make the Egg Sauce.

3. To serve, spoon the Egg Sauce over the salmon steaks and garnish each serving with a fresh dill sprig.

4 servings

Egg Sauce

This sauce also nicely complements baked or broiled fish. Just substitute half a cup of bottled clam juice or canned chicken broth for the poaching liquid.

3 tablespoons butter
¼ cup flour
½ cup poaching liquid, reserved from salmon
   recipe (above)
¼ cup canned chicken broth
½ cup heavy cream

Dash of salt
⅛ teaspoon pepper, preferably white
¼ cup finely chopped carrot
¼ cup finely chopped onion
2 hard-cooked eggs, coarsely chopped
2 tablespoons chopped fresh dill

1. In a medium saucepan, melt the butter over medium heat. Whisk in the flour. Stir in the reserved salmon poaching liquid, the chicken broth, and cream. Increase the heat to high and cook, stirring constantly, until the sauce comes to a boil, about 1 minute.

2. Whisk in the salt, pepper, carrot, and onion. Reduce the heat to low and simmer, stirring occasionally, for 10 minutes.

3. Gently stir in the eggs and the chopped dill.

Makes about 2 cups

ABOUT COUNTRY HAM

A southern-style country ham makes an impressive main course for a holiday dinner or a weekend supper. Its complex, smoky flavor is worth the extra time involved in its preparation.

Unlike the brine-cured hams sold in supermarkets, country hams, by definition, are produced with a dry cure of salt or a combination of salt, sugar, and nitrates. Once cured, the hams are aged, which reduces their moisture content by as much as 30 percent, and then usually smoked. Federal law requires that the combined curing and aging time for a country ham be at least 70 days.

The flavor of a country ham depends in part upon what feed the hog has been given. In Virginia, for example, acorns and peanuts are traditionally fed to hogs, while in Kentucky, clover and grain are preferred. Aging, which can take from three months to a year, also contributes to the flavor, and to the saltiness, firm texture, and rich color of the meat. The wood used for smoking—be it hickory, apple, or sassafras—adds its own particular aroma.

Smithfield ham, named for the small Virginia town where, by federal law, it must be cured, is the best-known country ham. Because of its popularity, Smithfield ham can be found in specialty food stores and butcher shops in many parts of the country; other less-known country hams are sold only by mail order.

Today most smokehouses offer both uncooked and fully cooked country hams. A whole country ham generally weighs between 13 and 18 pounds, but shank and butt halves

are usually also available. Cooked country ham generally comes vacuum packed, and can be eaten without further cooking. Uncooked country ham needs preparation. Don't be alarmed at the appearance of an uncooked, dry-cured country ham. Smithfield and other country hams are often smoke-blackened, encrusted with pepper, and occasionally lightly coated with mold. The mold, however, is a natural, desirable result of curing and aging.

Whether an uncooked country ham has mold or not, it benefits from soaking before it is cooked. Scrub the exterior of the ham with a stiff brush under warm running water. Then place the ham in a large pot with cold water to cover, and soak for 12 to 24 hours, changing the water at least twice. If you prefer a less salty ham, soak it for up to 48 hours.

To cook the ham, return it to the pot, cover with wine, beer, cider, or water, and add spices such as cloves or bay leaves. Slowly bring the liquid to a simmer and cook the ham for 15 to 20 minutes per pound, or until the shank bone can be moved easily in its socket. Drain the ham, and when it is cool enough to handle, remove the skin and all but ¼ inch of the fat. The ham may be eaten as is, or it may be baked, plain or glazed, in a 400° oven for about 20 minutes.

There are many ways to serve leftover country ham. Cut the meat into thin slices and offer them with buttermilk biscuits or cornbread. Or lay slices of ham over wedges of melon or fresh figs. Country ham is also delicious chopped and added to omelets or scalloped potatoes. And, of course, the bone can be used to add flavor to a hearty soup.

Maryland Crab Cakes

To be truly authentic, these crab cakes—a specialty of the Eastern Shore of Maryland—should be made with blue crabs from the Chesapeake Bay, although any crabmeat you use will produce mouth-watering results.

1 pound lump crabmeat, picked over to remove
    any bits of shell or cartilage
1 cup chopped scallions (about 5 medium)
1 slice firm-textured white bread, torn into large
    crumbs (about ½ cup)
¼ cup chopped parsley
2 eggs, lightly beaten

2 tablespoons mayonnaise
1 tablespoon Dijon mustard
2 teaspoons Worcestershire sauce
¼ teaspoon pepper
1 cup fine, dry breadcrumbs
About 4 tablespoons butter
Hot pepper sauce

1. In a large bowl, combine the crabmeat, scallions, large breadcrumbs, parsley, eggs, mayonnaise, mustard, Worcestershire sauce, and pepper. Shape the mixture into 12 cakes. Roll each cake in the dry breadcrumbs.

2. In a large skillet, melt 4 tablespoons of the butter over medium-high heat until just beginning to smoke. Carefully add the crab cakes, in batches, and cook until browned on one side, 2 to 3 minutes. Gently turn the cakes and cook until browned on the second side, 2 to 3 minutes longer. Add more butter if necessary to prevent sticking.

3. Serve the crab cakes hot, with the hot pepper sauce on the side.   *4 servings*

Red Flannel Hash

Hash is the quintessential comfort food, and red flannel hash—which gets its colorful name and appearance from beets—is a classic. It is also a perfect candidate for using up leftovers from the New England Boiled Dinner (page 37). To make this substantial dish even heartier, cook eggs on top of the hash at the end of Step 4: Make four indents in the hash with the back of a spoon. Break an egg into each indentation, cover the skillet, and cook until the eggs are set.

The corned beef, potato, and beet mixture used to make red flannel hash also makes a delicious shepherd's pie. Prepare the hash through Step 3, place it in a baking dish, and cover with a layer of fresh, hot mashed potatoes. Gloss the top of the mashed potatoes with a little melted butter, then bake in a 400° oven until the potatoes are browned.

1 pound boiling potatoes, peeled and cut into ½-inch cubes
3 small beets, peeled and cut into ½-inch cubes
1¾ cups diced cooked corned beef
1 small onion, chopped
½ cup diced green bell pepper
¼ cup chopped parsley
¼ cup heavy cream
4 teaspoons Worcestershire sauce
1 teaspoon salt
¼ teaspoon black pepper
4 to 6 tablespoons butter

1. In separate saucepans of boiling water, cook the potatoes and beets until tender, 10 to 15 minutes. Drain well.

2. In a large bowl, mix together the potatoes, beets, corned beef, onion, green pepper, parsley, cream, Worcestershire sauce, salt, and black pepper.

3. In a large skillet, melt 4 tablespoons of the butter over medium-high heat. Add the hash and cook, stirring frequently, until golden brown, about 10 minutes. Add up to 2 tablespoons more butter if necessary to prevent sticking.

4. Press the mixture down lightly to form a cake and continue cooking until the bottom has browned, about 5 minutes.

5. Remove the hash from the pan and serve hot. *4 servings*

Barbecued Spareribs with Orange Sauce

The term finger-lickin' must certainly have been invented by someone who had been eating barbecued spareribs, a dish that is usually covered with a sticky (though delicious) sauce and that absolutely must be eaten with the fingers. Serve these spareribs with corn biscuits, a coleslaw (such as Tart Red and Green Coleslaw, page 104), and cold beer. To make the spareribs a bit leaner, parboil them first (see Note) to cook off some of the fat.

2 cups ketchup
1 cup orange marmalade
2 tablespoons tomato paste
2 tablespoons Dijon mustard
2 tablespoons Worcestershire sauce
1 medium onion, minced (about 1¼ cups)
2 cloves garlic, minced
2 slabs lean spareribs (about 3½ pounds)

1. In a medium saucepan, bring the ketchup, marmalade, tomato paste, mustard, Worcestershire sauce, onion, and garlic to a boil over medium-high heat. Reduce

Barbecued Spareribs with Orange Sauce

the heat to medium-low and simmer, partially covered, for 30 minutes, stirring occasionally.

2. Preheat the oven to 375°.

3. Place the spareribs, meaty-side up, on a foil-lined baking pan. Brush the spareribs with one-third of the barbecue sauce and bake for 20 minutes.

4. Turn the spareribs over, coat with half the remaining barbecue sauce, and bake for another 20 minutes.

5. Turn the spareribs meaty-side up again, coat with the remaining barbecue sauce, and bake for 20 minutes longer.

6. Cut the spareribs into serving pieces and serve hot or cold.   *6 to 8 servings*

NOTE: To parboil the spareribs, bring a large stockpot two-thirds full of water to a boil. Add the spareribs and cook for 4 minutes.

Grillades and Grits

Grillades and grits is a real down-home Louisiana dish in which meat, usually veal, is braised in a rich tomatoey gravy and then served over hominy grits. Although it is traditionally served at breakfast, this dish is extremely hearty and would make a satisfying main course for lunch or dinner.

¼ pound bacon (4 to 6 slices)
4 boneless veal round steaks, cut ½ inch thick
   (about ¼ pound each)
⅓ cup flour
1½ teaspoons salt
¼ teaspoon black pepper
1 medium red onion, chopped (about 1⅔ cups)
1 small yellow or green bell pepper, chopped
   (about ⅔ cup)
1 stalk celery, chopped (about ½ cup)
2 cloves garlic, minced

1 can (14 ounces) whole tomatoes,
   with their juice
2 tablespoons tomato paste
2 teaspoons Worcestershire sauce
2 teaspoons red wine vinegar
½ teaspoon basil
¼ teaspoon crushed red pepper
1 bay leaf
5 cups water
1 cup hominy grits

1. In a large skillet, cook the bacon over medium heat until crisp, about 10 minutes. Reserving the fat in the pan, drain the bacon on paper towels; crumble and set aside.

2. Pat the veal steaks dry. In a shallow bowl, mix together the flour, ½ teaspoon of the salt, and the black pepper. Dredge the veal in the seasoned flour and shake off any excess.

3. Heat the bacon fat in the skillet over moderate heat until hot but not smoking. Add the veal steaks and brown on both sides, 2 to 3 minutes per side. Remove the veal to a platter and cover loosely with foil to keep warm.

4. In the fat remaining in the skillet, sauté the onion, bell pepper, celery, and garlic over medium heat until the vegetables are softened but not browned, about 10 minutes. Stir in the tomatoes with their juice, the tomato paste, Worcestershire sauce, vinegar, basil, red pepper, bay leaf, and ½ teaspoon of the salt.

5. Add the veal steaks, increase the heat to high, and bring the liquid to a boil. Reduce the heat to low and simmer, partially covered, turning the steaks occasionally, until the veal is tender when pierced with a knife, about 1 hour. Discard the bay leaf.

6. About 30 minutes before the veal is done, in a medium saucepan, bring the water and the remaining ½ teaspoon salt to a boil. Stirring constantly, pour the grits in slowly so that the water keeps boiling. Reduce the heat to low, cover tightly, and simmer, stirring occasionally, for 15 to 20 minutes. Remove from the heat and let stand, covered, a few minutes (the grits will continue to cook and get firmer as they stand).

7. To serve, place a veal steak on a mound of grits and top with pan gravy and crumbled bacon.

4 servings

Chicken with Parsley Dumplings

The light, airy parsley-flecked dumplings served with this poached chicken lend a delicate note to an otherwise humble dish.

3-pound chicken, rinsed
4 cups canned chicken broth
About 6 cups water
1 medium onion, quartered
2 medium carrots
2 stalks celery
10 sprigs parsley
1 bay leaf
1½ cups flour

7 tablespoons butter, softened to room
*   temperature*
2 teaspoons baking powder
¾ teaspoon salt
¼ teaspoon pepper
2 tablespoons chopped parsley
¼ cup milk
1 egg, lightly beaten
1 cup chopped scallions (about 5 medium)

1. In a Dutch oven or flameproof casserole, place the chicken, chicken broth, 6 cups of water, onion, carrots, celery, parsley sprigs, and bay leaf. Add more water, if necessary, to cover the chicken completely. Bring to a boil over medium-high heat. Reduce the heat to medium-low, cover, and simmer until the chicken is tender, about 45 minutes.

2. Remove the chicken to a serving platter and discard the broth vegetables. Skim any fat from the surface of the broth, measure out 6 cups of broth, and reserve the remainder for another use. The chicken can be left whole, cut into serving pieces, or, when cool enough to handle, the meat can be removed from the bone. Arrange the chicken on a serving platter and cover loosely with foil to keep warm.

3. In a small bowl, with your fingertips, thoroughly blend ¼ cup of the flour with 4 tablespoons of the butter. In a large saucepan, bring the 6 cups of broth to a boil over medium-high heat. Pinch off pieces of the flour-butter mixture and drop them, one at a time, into the broth, stirring to incorporate after each addition Reduce the heat to medium-low and let the sauce simmer while you make the dumplings.

4. Make the dumplings: In a bowl, combine the remaining 1¼ cups flour with the baking powder, salt, and pepper. Cut in the remaining 3 tablespoons butter until the mixture resembles coarse meal. Stir in the chopped parsley. Add the milk and beaten egg, and blend to form a soft dough.

5. Increase the heat under the sauce to medium-high and bring to a boil. Drop the dumpling dough, a tablespoon at a time, into the broth. Reduce the heat to medium-low, cover, and simmer for 10 minutes.

6. Just before serving, stir in the scallions. Spoon the dumplings and some of the sauce around the chicken on the serving platter. Pass any remaining sauce separately.

4 servings

A Meal from the Hearth

Hearth cooking—that is, cooking in a fireplace or "down hearth" (on the brick apron of the fireplace)—is a good way to re-create a part of America's past. Until the advent of wood-burning cookstoves in the 1850s, the hearth was where most meals were prepared. While today cooking at the hearth is too time-consuming for an everyday meal, it is an unusual and rewarding way to entertain family and friends.

Some basic equipment is required for successful hearth cookery. If your fireplace is large enough, you may want to install a swinging crane—a hinged device that is bolted to one side of the fireplace and from which pots can be suspended by means of trammels, hooks, and hangers. Although a crane is not necessary for preparing the recipes on the following pages, you will need durable cookware made of cast iron, tinned copper, or lined brass. A large and small spider (long-handled frying pan with three legs), a few posnets (three-legged saucepans), a tin reflector oven, and a wafer iron are the utensils used here, but you can substitute more common cookware, as noted on page 55. Long-handled spoons, spatulas, and forks are also essential, and, for the fire, a poker, tongs, and a shovel.

Safety in hearth cookery is of the utmost importance. Wear natural fibers, sturdy shoes, a kerchief or hat to protect your hair, and long mitts to shield your arms. Keep a water bucket, fire blanket, and fire extinguisher near the fireplace.

Direct flames are needed for boiling water; otherwise most hearth cookery is done over hot coals. To be sure that you have enough coals for preparing a meal such as this one, start the fire about two hours before you plan to cook. Use newspaper, kindling, and dry, well-seasoned wood to build a fire in the fireplace. Hardwoods, such as oak or any of the various fruit and nut woods, which burn slowly and add flavor to the food, are best.

Once you have a quantity of coals, rake or shovel them into three or four small piles on the hearth apron; your spider or posnet should sit several inches above the coals. How fast the food cooks depends on the heat generated, the thickness of the cookware, and how far the cookware is from the coals. Additional heat can be created by adding more embers; less heat by removing some coals from the piles. You should watch your pots constantly and adjust the heat as necessary.

Learning how to regulate the heat and understanding the conducting properties of your cookware will take time and require experimentation. Once you have learned to control these variables, you will find that cooking times for hearth cookery are often the same as for food cooked in the oven or on the stove.

Ducks with currant-port glaze, corn fritters, and spinach cook on the hearth. Wafers will be made in a wafer iron for dessert. See the recipes that follow.

All of these recipes have been adapted from 18th- and 19th-century cookbooks. Be sure to start the fire at least two hours before you want to begin cooking so that you have enough coals. Measure out all the ingredients and set them on a table near the fireplace; then everything will be at hand when you are ready to cook.

Once the embers are red-hot, start cooking the ducks; about 15 minutes before they are done, prepare the corn fritters. While the ducks rest before carving, simmer the spinach. After dinner you can invite your guests to help make the wafers.

Consult historical cookbooks and books on hearth cookery for additional recipes and tips.

This elegant meal from the hearth features slices of succulent, smoky-flavored duck served with corn fritters (sometimes called corn oysters) and spinach on toast points.

ROAST DUCK WITH CURRANT-PORT GLAZE

1 tablespoon butter
1 medium onion, chopped
2 tablespoons minced fresh sage, or 1 teaspoon dried
Salt and pepper, to taste
2 ducklings (4 to 6 pounds each), rinsed and patted dry, giblets trimmed and set aside

One 1-inch-thick slice French or Italian country bread
¾ cup Port wine
½ cup currant jelly

1. In small posnet or spider, melt butter over medium-hot embers. Add onion, sage, salt, and pepper, and sauté until onions are softened but not browned. Rub half the mixture into cavity of each duck. Wipe pan clean.

2. Soak bread in ½ cup of the wine until it softens, then add half the bread to cavity of each duck. Rub ducks all over with salt and pepper.

3. Place both ducks on spit of reflector oven, balancing them evenly. Skewer to hold ducks in place and truss with kitchen twine. Place spit in reflector oven and set oven about 8 to 12 inches from hot embers. Roast ducks for about 20 minutes per pound, turning spit setting every 10 to 15 minutes so that ducks cook evenly, and carefully draining fat from bottom of oven as necessary. About 10 minutes before ducks are done, move reflector oven to within 6 inches of hot embers and brush ducks with half the currant jelly. Reserve remaining jelly. Ducks are done when skin is browned and juices run yellow when thigh is pricked with fork.

4. About 30 minutes before ducks are done, make gravy. Chop giblets and place in same pan in which you cooked onions. Set pan over medium-hot embers and add just enough water to cover giblets. Simmer until tender, about 30 minutes, adding more water as necessary. Move pan over hot embers and stir in remaining ¼ cup wine and currant jelly. Cook until gravy thickens. Season with salt and pepper. Keep gravy warm.

5. When ducks are done, remove from spit, cut string, and, with spoon, remove onion-bread mixture from cavities. Add to giblet gravy, stirring until well blended. Keep gravy warm. Let ducks rest, loosely covered, on warm platter for 15 minutes before carving.   4 to 6 servings

◆

CORN FRITTERS

4 cups fresh corn kernels, or 4 cups frozen, thawed
4 eggs, beaten
4 tablespoons flour
¼ cup heavy cream

Salt and pepper, to taste
2 cups maple syrup, for topping
3 tablespoons butter

1. In large mixing bowl, combine corn, eggs, flour, cream, salt, and pepper. Stir until corn kernels are evenly coated with batter.

2. Pour syrup into small posnet and warm over low embers.

3. Meanwhile, place 10-inch spider over hot embers. Add butter to pan and heat until test drop of batter sizzles on contact.

4. Drop batter into pan by large spoonfuls, taking care not to crowd fritters. Cook fritters for a few minutes on each side, turning once, until both sides are golden brown. Drain on paper towels. Keep fritters warm on heated platter while preparing remaining fritters.

5. Drizzle warm maple syrup over fritters and serve.   4 servings

SPINACH ON TOAST POINTS

1 pound fresh spinach,
    trimmed
Salt and pepper, to taste
4 slices white bread,
    crusts removed

1 tablespoon butter,
    plus butter for toast
2 teaspoons flour
1 egg yolk, beaten

1. Wash spinach well and drain, allowing some water to cling to leaves.

2. Put spinach in small posnet. Add salt and pepper and cook slowly over low embers, stirring often, and pressing with wooden spoon to release moisture, until spinach is tender.

3. Transfer spinach to colander and press again with spoon to release moisture. Chop spinach fine.

4. Toast bread in rotary toaster over low embers. Cut toast into 8 triangles, butter them lightly, and keep warm.

5. In small bowl, use fingertips to blend 1 tablespoon butter with flour. Return spinach to pan, set over low embers, and stir in flour-butter mixture. Add egg yolk and simmer, stirring constantly so that egg does not curdle, until spinach-egg mixture is hot and thickened, about 5 minutes.

6. Mound spinach on toast points and serve.   4 servings

◆

DESSERT WAFERS

1½ sticks (6 ounces) butter
4 eggs
1 cup sugar
½ teaspoon grated lemon zest
⅛ teaspoon salt

1 to 1½ cups flour
Whipped cream and jam, for
    topping
Powdered sugar (optional)

1. In small posnet, melt butter over low embers. Set aside and keep warm.

2. In medium mixing bowl, beat eggs and sugar together. Stir in ½ cup of the melted butter, lemon zest, and salt. Add enough flour to make stiff batter.

3. Preheat wafer iron over hot embers. Turn to heat both sides. Open iron on flat surface. Dip corner of clean cloth into remaining melted butter and use cloth to grease both sides of iron. To test heat of iron, spoon about 1 teaspoon batter into iron and close. If batter sizzles, iron is hot enough. Place iron back over hot embers, and after about 30 seconds, open it. If batter seems too runny, add a little more flour to mixture and repeat test.

4. To make wafers, spoon some batter inside iron (amount will depend on size of iron), close iron quickly but gently, and place over hot embers, propping handle on a log. Cooking time will vary, depending on heat of embers and thickness of iron. Open iron after 30 seconds, however, to check wafer for doneness; it should be golden, not brown. If wafer is not done, close iron again and continue cooking. When wafer is done, rest iron on flat surface, open, and remove wafer with dull knife. To serve wafer rolled, roll immediately; after cooling, it will be brittle.

5. Cook remaining batter in same manner, reheating iron for each wafer and greasing it after every other wafer, or as needed.

6. Serve wafers topped or filled with jam and whipped cream. Or dust with powdered sugar, if desired.

Makes about 2 dozen, allowing for breakage and mistakes

SPECIAL EQUIPMENT

For the duck:
· Small posnet or small spider, or small cast-iron skillet and trivet
· Reflector oven with spit and skewers

For the corn fritters:
· Small posnet, or small saucepan and cast-iron trivet
· 10-inch spider, or large cast-iron skillet and trivet

For the spinach:
· Small posnet, or small open kettle and cast-iron trivet
· Rotary toaster or long fork

For the wafers:
· Small posnet, or small saucepan and cast-iron trivet
· Wafer iron with long handle

Wafers that taste like ice cream cones, topped or filled with jam and whipped cream, are a delicious dessert. For the best results, have two people work together at the hearth to make the wafers.

Roast Duck with Cranberry, Apricot, and Sausage Stuffing

Tart fruits such as cranberries and apricots are natural partners for the rich, meaty flavor of roast duck. This recipe uses fresh cranberries and apricot preserves in both the stuffing and the sauce. To give the stuffing a slightly different flavor and texture, make it with brown rice instead of white rice.

Wild duck is a delicious alternative to domestic duck. Remember that wild ducks weigh only about 2 pounds and that it takes just 20 minutes to roast one at 450°. One bird feeds two people.

STUFFING
1 tablespoon butter
1 clove garlic, minced
½ pound pork sausage, casings removed
1 cup chopped scallions (about 5 medium)
1 cup chopped celery (about 2 stalks)
¾ cup fresh cranberries
½ cup apricot preserves
2 tablespoons chopped parsley
¾ teaspoon thyme
½ teaspoon salt
¼ teaspoon pepper
3 cups cooked rice

DUCK AND SAUCE
5-pound duckling, rinsed
Juice of ½ lemon (about 2 tablespoons)
1 teaspoon salt
2 tablespoons butter
¼ cup chopped shallots (2 to 3 medium),
    or ¼ cup chopped onion
1 clove garlic, minced
1 cup fresh cranberries
½ cup apricot preserves

1. Preheat the oven to 475°.

2. Make the stuffing: In a large skillet, melt the butter over medium-high heat. Add the garlic and sausage, and sauté, breaking up the meat with a spoon, for 5 minutes.

3. Add the scallions, celery, cranberries, apricot preserves, parsley, thyme, salt, and pepper, and cook, stirring, for 10 minutes longer.

4. Stir in the rice. There should be about 7 cups of stuffing.

5. Prepare the duck: Remove the giblets and reserve for another use. Remove the excess fat from the duck and fill the cavity loosely with about half of the stuffing. Place the remaining stuffing in a greased baking dish, cover, and set aside. Truss the duck, rub with the lemon juice, and sprinkle with the salt. Prick the duck all over with a fork and place it, breast-side up, on a rack in a roasting pan.

6. Roast the duck for 15 minutes. Lower the oven temperature to 350° and continue roasting, drawing off the fat occasionally, until the duck is golden brown and an instant-reading meat thermometer inserted into the thickest part of the leg registers 180°, about 1½ hours. About 30 minutes before the duck is done, place the baking dish of stuffing in the oven and bake.

7. Make the sauce: In a small saucepan, melt the butter over medium heat. Add the shallots and garlic, and sauté for 5 minutes. Add the cranberries and apricot preserves, reduce the heat to medium-low, and cook for 5 minutes. Let the mixture cool slightly and then purée it in a food processor or blender.

8. Serve the duck with the stuffing and the sauce on the side.   *4 to 6 servings*

Roast Duck with Cranberry, Apricot, and Sausage Stuffing

Hangtown Fry

Hangtown Fry

Legend has it that a Gold Rush miner who had recently hit pay dirt walked into a restaurant in Hangtown (now called Placerville), California, and asked for the most expensive dish in the place. The kitchen responded with this egg-and-oyster extravaganza, which was expensive not because of the oysters, but the eggs.

¼ pound bacon (4 to 6 slices)	*2 tablespoons milk*
12 unsalted saltine crackers, finely crushed	*½ pint shucked oysters, drained and patted dry*
¼ cup flour	*2 tablespoons butter*
½ teaspoon salt	*2 tablespoons chopped parsley*
⅜ teaspoon pepper	*1 tablespoon chopped chives (optional)*
6 eggs	*1 lemon, cut into wedges*

1. In a large skillet, cook the bacon over medium heat until crisp, about 10 minutes. Reserving the fat in the pan, drain the bacon on paper towels. Crumble and set it aside.

2. In a shallow bowl, mix together the cracker crumbs, flour, and ¼ teaspoon each of the salt and pepper. In another bowl, beat 1 of the eggs with the milk. Dip the oysters first in the egg-milk mixture and then dredge in the crumb-flour mixture. Reserve the remaining egg-milk mixture.

3. Melt the butter in the bacon fat over medium heat. Add the oysters and sauté until golden on all sides, 2 to 4 minutes.

4. Meanwhile, in a bowl, beat the remaining 5 eggs with the reserved egg-milk mixture, the parsley, chives (if using), and the remaining ¼ teaspoon salt and ⅛ teaspoon pepper.

5. Pour the egg mixture over the oysters in the pan. Cook the eggs, lifting with a spatula to allow uncooked egg to flow underneath, until they are set, 3 to 4 minutes.

6. Sprinkle with the crumbled bacon and serve with lemon wedges.   *4 servings*

Chicken-Fried Steak with Tomato Gravy

Here is real American roadside diner food. Popular all across the West and Southwest, steak that is "chicken-fried" is dredged in flour and/or cracker crumbs and cooked in hot oil—just like fried chicken. By tradition, the meat used in this dish is on the inexpensive side.

*4 boneless round steaks (about ½ pound each
  and cut ½ inch thick), halved*
¾ cup flour
2 eggs
2 tablespoons milk
*12 unsalted saltine crackers,
  finely crushed*

1½ teaspoons salt
½ teaspoon pepper
1 cup peanut oil
1 cup light cream or half-and-half
1 large tomato, chopped (about 1½ cups)
1 teaspoon Worcestershire sauce
2 tablespoons chopped parsley

1. Dredge the steaks in ¼ cup of the flour; set aside. Discard any unused flour.

2. In a shallow bowl, beat the eggs with the milk. In another shallow bowl, combine the remaining ½ cup flour with the cracker crumbs and add 1 teaspoon of the salt and all of the pepper. Dip the steaks in the egg mixture and then in the seasoned flour-crumb mixture. Reserve the excess flour-crumb mixture. Set the steaks aside on a pastry rack.

3. In a large skillet, heat the oil over medium-high heat until hot but not smoking. In batches, add the steaks and brown well, about 2 minutes per side. Transfer to a platter and cover loosely with foil to keep warm.

4. Pour off all but 3 tablespoons of oil. Over medium heat, stir in 3 tablespoons of the reserved flour-crumb mixture, scraping up any browned bits from the bottom and sides of the skillet. Stir in the cream and cook until slightly thickened, 1 to 2 minutes. Stir in the tomato, Worcestershire sauce, chopped parsley, and the remaining ½ teaspoon salt.

5. Serve the steaks topped with the tomato gravy.   *4 servings*

Housekeeping in Old Virginia, *a cookbook from 1877, offers these instructions for fattening oysters at home: "Mix one pint of salt with thirty pints of water. Put the oysters in a tub that will not leak, with their mouths upwards and feed them with the above, by dipping in a broom and frequently passing over their mouths. It is said that they will fatten still more by mixing fine meal with the water."*

Pork Chops with Sausage-Apple Stuffing

Instead of the usual stuffed pork chop recipe, in which a pocket is cut into the side of the chop and then filled with some of the stuffing mixture, this simplified version calls for cooking the "stuffing" separately and serving it with the pork chops as a side dish. This method not only makes the recipe simpler, but also gives hungry guests the opportunity to have a more substantial portion of the tasty sausage-apple stuffing.

¼ cup flour

¼ teaspoon salt

⅛ teaspoon pepper

4 center-cut loin pork chops (about ½ pound each and cut 1 inch thick)

1 to 2 tablespoons olive oil

1½ cups plus 1 tablespoon apple cider

½ teaspoon crumbled sage

1 tablespoon butter

2 Italian sweet sausages (about 3 ounces each), casings removed

1 small onion, chopped (about ½ cup)

1 clove garlic, minced

½ tart green apple, such as Granny Smith, unpeeled and chopped (about ⅔ cup)

1 slice firm-textured white bread, torn into crumbs (about ½ cup)

¼ cup heavy cream

2 tablespoons chopped parsley, for garnish

1. In a shallow bowl, combine the flour, salt, and pepper. Dredge the pork chops in the seasoned flour, tapping off any excess.

2. In a large skillet, heat 1 tablespoon of the oil over medium-high heat. Add the pork chops and brown quickly on both sides, adding another tablespoon of oil if necessary to prevent sticking.

3. Pour the fat from the skillet. Add 1½ cups of the cider and ¼ teaspoon of the sage, cover, and simmer over medium-low heat until the chops are tender, about 40 minutes.

4. About 20 minutes before the chops are done, in a separate large skillet, melt the butter over medium-high heat. Add the sausage meat, breaking it up with a spoon. Add the onion and garlic, and cook until the meat begins to brown, about 5 minutes. Add the apple, breadcrumbs, and the remaining 1 tablespoon cider and ¼ teaspoon sage, and continue cooking, stirring frequently, until the apple is tender, 5 to 10 minutes.

5. When the pork chops are cooked, remove them from the skillet and cover loosely with foil to keep warm. Add the cream to the cooking juices in the pan and cook over medium-high heat until the sauce has thickened slightly, 2 to 3 minutes.

6. To serve, place a pork chop on each plate and top with some of the sausage-apple mixture. Cover with sauce and garnish with the chopped parsley.

4 servings

Southern Fried Chicken with Cream Gravy

What produces the perfect fried chicken has long been an issue in American country cooking. Southerners continue to argue about what to dip the chicken in, what to dredge it in, and what fat to fry it in. Although all cooks have their own formula for success, most would probably agree that the skillet you use should be cast iron, and the fat you fry in should be good and hot.

2½ pounds chicken parts, rinsed and patted dry	*About 4 cups peanut oil, for frying*
1 cup buttermilk	*2 tablespoons butter*
1 cup flour	*1 cup light cream or half-and-half*
2 teaspoons paprika	*1 cup milk*
1¼ teaspoons salt	*2 teaspoons dry sherry*
¾ teaspoon pepper	*2 tablespoons chopped parsley*

1. Place the chicken in a large nonreactive bowl and toss with the buttermilk to coat. Let the chicken marinate for at least 15 minutes.

2. In another large bowl, combine the flour, paprika, 1 teaspoon of the salt, and ½ teaspoon of the pepper. In a large cast iron skillet, heat ½ inch of oil to 375° over medium-high heat.

3. Dredge the chicken well in the seasoned flour. Remove the chicken and reserve the dredging flour. Add the chicken, skin-side down, in batches if necessary, to the skillet. Reduce the heat to medium, cover, and fry for 15 minutes.

4. Turn the chicken over, and cook, uncovered, until it is golden brown and the internal temperature registers 180° on an instant-reading meat thermometer, 10 to 15 minutes longer. Remove the chicken and drain on paper towels.

5. Carefully pour the oil into a heatproof container. Return 2 tablespoons of the oil to the skillet, add the butter, and heat over medium heat. Add ¼ cup of the reserved dredging flour and cook, stirring constantly, until the flour is browned, 2 to 3 minutes. Stir in the cream and milk, and slowly bring to a boil. Reduce the heat to medium-low and simmer, uncovered, for 5 minutes. Stir in the sherry, parsley, and remaining ¼ teaspoon salt and ¼ teaspoon pepper.

6. Serve the chicken hot with the gravy on the side. *4 servings*

Stews and Casseroles

*simple, heartwarming
country food*

🍃

Stews and casseroles are perhaps the most satisfying form of country cooking. Both offer endless possibilities for combining ingredients and both require relatively little labor in the kitchen. Depending on their origins, stews and casseroles are known by many other names: burgoos, muddles, stratas, and gumbos among them.

Stews have been a staple in country cooking since the first settlers arrived. A colonial housewife would simply put whatever she had into a pot, hang the pot on a crane over the fire, and attend to her chores, returning to the hearth occasionally to stir the mixture. This method of slow cooking was ideal for tenderizing tough meat, a boon since most early Americans did not have a full set of teeth. Today the mark of a great stew is not how long it is cooked but the freshness of the ingredients.

It was not until the 1950s that the casserole became popular as a timesaving dish. The recipes that follow feature some new twists on some old standbys: macaroni is enhanced with three cheeses, tuna casserole is made with fresh tuna, and a cheese strata is enlivened with broccoli florets.

Fresh ingredients are the secret to a successful lamb stew.

Baked Macaroni with Three Cheeses

Although many people think of macaroni and cheese as a dish that originated in the 1950s, it actually dates back to the early 19th century. If you can't find white Cheddar, simply increase the amount of yellow to half a pound.

2 cups elbow macaroni
1 stick (4 ounces) butter
1 medium onion, chopped (about 1¼ cups)
1 clove garlic, minced
⅓ cup flour
2 cups milk
1 to 2 tablespoons Dijon mustard
2 teaspoons Worcestershire sauce
1 cup grated Swiss cheese (about ¼ pound)

1 cup grated sharp white Cheddar cheese
  (about ¼ pound)
1 cup grated yellow Cheddar cheese (about
  ¼ pound)
½ cup sour cream
3 stalks celery, diced (about 1½ cups)
½ pound ham, cut into ½-inch cubes (about
  1½ cups)
2 tablespoons chopped parsley, for garnish

*M*ost noodle casseroles *freeze well. Just remember to stop cooking five to ten minutes before the casserole is done so it will not overcook when it is reheated. Before reheating, add a little liquid, since the freezing process often causes a dish to lose some moisture.*

1. Preheat the oven to 375°. Butter a 2½-quart casserole or baking dish.

2. In a large saucepan of boiling salted water, cook the macaroni according to package directions until tender but still firm. Drain well, and set aside.

3. In a medium saucepan, melt the butter over medium heat. Add the onion and garlic, and sauté until the onion is softened but not browned, about 10 minutes.

4. Stir in the flour until a paste is formed. Whisk in the milk, mustard, and Worcestershire sauce, and bring to a boil. Reduce the heat to medium-low and continue cooking, stirring constantly, until the sauce is thickened, 2 to 4 minutes.

5. Remove the pan from the heat and stir in the Swiss and the white and yellow Cheddar cheeses. Then stir in the sour cream, celery, ham cubes, and the reserved macaroni.

6. Turn the mixture into the prepared casserole, cover tightly with foil, and bake for 20 minutes, or until hot and bubbly. Uncover and bake 5 minutes longer, or until the top browns lightly. Sprinkle with the parsley before serving.   *6 to 8 servings*

Virginia Chicken Pudding

This colonial chicken dish was one of President James Monroe's favorites. Lest you think that he had odd taste in desserts, the pudding referred to is Yorkshire pudding: an egg-rich batter is poured over the chicken, and then both are baked until the chicken is done and the pudding is puffed and golden brown.

1¾ cups flour
1 teaspoon salt
¼ teaspoon pepper
2½ pounds chicken parts, rinsed and patted dry
4 tablespoons butter

1 cup peanut oil
3 eggs
1 cup milk
2 tablespoons chopped parsley, for
  garnish

Virginia Chicken Pudding

1. In a shallow bowl, combine ½ cup of the flour, ½ teaspoon of the salt, and the pepper. Add the chicken pieces and dredge well in the seasoned flour.

2. In a large skillet, melt the butter in the oil over medium-high heat. Add the chicken and fry until golden brown, about 5 minutes per side. Drain on paper towels.

3. Preheat the oven to 450°.

4. Transfer the chicken to a buttered shallow baking dish or gratin dish big enough to hold the chicken snugly in one layer (about an 11 x 8 x 1½-inch dish).

5. In a bowl, combine the remaining 1¼ cups flour and ½ teaspoon salt. In another bowl, beat the eggs until frothy and add the milk. Beat the egg-milk mixture into the flour and stir until the batter is smooth.

6. Pour the batter evenly over the chicken and place immediately in the oven. Bake for 15 minutes. Lower the oven temperature to 350° and bake for 20 to 25 minutes longer, or until the pudding puffs up and browns.

7. Serve the chicken hot, sprinkled with the parsley. *4 servings*

Tamale Pie

All of the ingredients for a typical beef tamale are combined in this delicious Southwestern casserole. For a simple variation, use Monterey Jack cheese instead of Cheddar.

4 tablespoons butter
2 cloves garlic, minced
1 medium onion, chopped (about 1¼ cups)
1 pound ground beef chuck
1 large green bell pepper, chopped (about 1½ cups)
1 cup corn kernels, fresh (about 2 ears) or frozen
1 can (14 ounces) whole tomatoes, drained
1 tablespoon tomato paste

2 tablespoons chili powder
1 teaspoon ground cumin
1½ teaspoons salt
2½ cups milk
¾ cup yellow cornmeal
2 cups grated Cheddar cheese (about ½ pound)
¼ pound fresh plum tomatoes, thinly sliced
½ cup chopped scallions (2 to 3 medium)

1. Preheat the oven to 350°. Butter a 2-quart casserole or soufflé dish.
2. In a large skillet, melt 2 tablespoons of the butter over medium-high heat. Add the garlic, onion, and ground beef, and cook, stirring occasionally, until the onion is softened and the beef begins to brown, about 10 minutes.

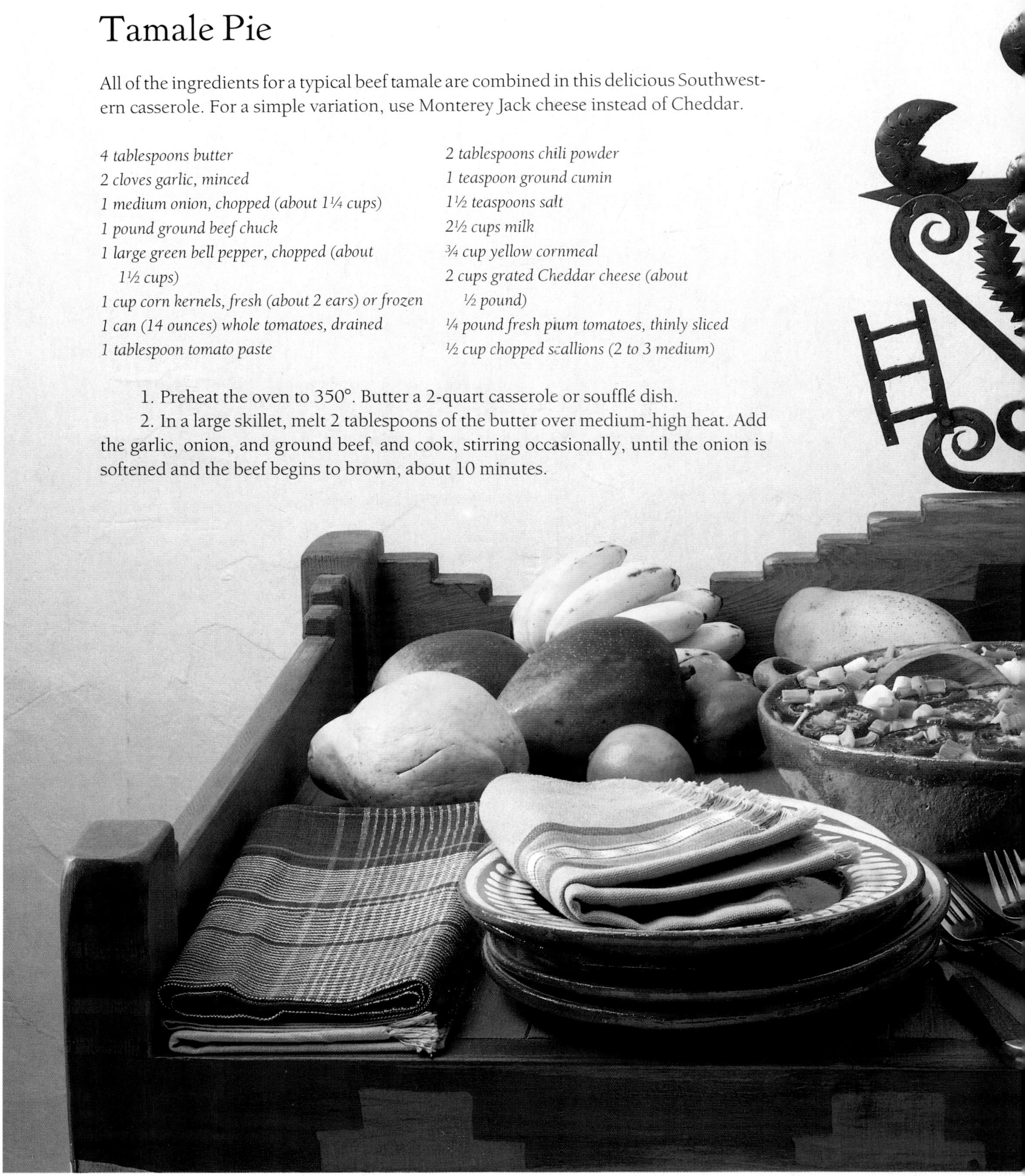

3. Stir in the green pepper, corn, canned tomatoes, tomato paste, chili powder, cumin, and 1 teaspoon of the salt. Reduce the heat to medium-low and simmer, uncovered, for about 10 minutes.

4. Meanwhile, in a medium saucepan, bring the milk almost to a boil over medium heat. Add the remaining 2 tablespoons butter and ½ teaspoon salt. Whisking constantly, gradually add the cornmeal. Reduce the heat to medium-low and simmer for 5 minutes. Remove from the heat and stir in 1 cup of the cheese.

5. Line the sides and bottom of the prepared casserole with two-thirds of the cornmeal mixture. Pour in the meat filling and top with the remaining cornmeal mixture, spreading it evenly.

6. Sprinkle the remaining 1 cup cheese on top. Arrange the fresh tomato slices over the cheese. Bake, uncovered, for 40 minutes.

7. Sprinkle the scallions on top and bake for 5 minutes longer.   *6 servings*

Shrimp and Chicken Pilau

The first thing you need to know about this South Carolina favorite is how to pronounce it. Although the name of the dish can be spelled any number of ways—pilau, perleau, pullao, pilaf, pilaw, and perlew among them—it is almost always pronounced "per-loo." This rice dish exists in similar forms all across the South, but it has its roots in the coastal Carolinas (where rice was once a major crop), and in Charleston in particular. The city was a busy seaport on the trade route to the Orient, where the original pilaus came from.

6 cups water
1 bay leaf
2½ pounds chicken parts, rinsed
¼ pound bacon (4 to 6 slices)
1 cup chopped scallions (about 5 medium)
1 medium green bell pepper, chopped (about 1 cup)
2 cloves garlic, minced
1½ cups raw rice

1 can (14 ounces) whole tomatoes, with their juice
2 teaspoons Worcestershire sauce
1 teaspoon thyme
1¼ teaspoons salt
½ teaspoon black pepper
1 pound medium shrimp, shelled and deveined
¼ cup chopped parsley, for garnish

1. Preheat the oven to 375°. Butter a 2-quart baking dish.

2. In a large saucepan, bring the water and bay leaf to a boil. Add the chicken, reduce the heat to medium-low, and cook, uncovered, until the chicken is tender, about 30 minutes. Remove the chicken, and when it is cool enough to handle, remove the meat from the bone, cut into bite-size pieces, and set aside. Measure out 1¾ cups of the poaching broth and set aside. Reserve the remaining broth for another use or discard.

3. In a large skillet, cook the bacon over medium heat until crisp, about 10 minutes. Reserving the fat in the pan, drain the bacon on paper towels; crumble and set aside.

4. In the bacon fat, sauté the scallions, green pepper, and garlic over medium heat for 5 minutes. Stir in the rice and cook, stirring, 5 minutes longer. Stir in the chicken and transfer to the prepared baking dish.

5. In a large saucepan, bring the tomatoes with their juice, Worcestershire sauce, thyme, salt, and black pepper to a boil. Pour over the mixture in the baking dish. Cover with foil and bake for 30 minutes.

6. Stir in the shrimp, re-cover, and bake for 10 minutes longer. Stir the mixture again, re-cover, and bake for 10 minutes longer, or until the rice is tender and has absorbed all the liquid.

7. Serve hot, topped with the parsley and crumbled bacon.   *6 servings*

Joe Booker Stew

Nobody remembers who Joe Booker was, yet his name endures in this hearty stew with dumplings, which is still very popular in Boothbay Harbor, Maine, where it is said to have originated. Veal is called for in this recipe, but beef can be used instead.

½ pound salt pork, cut into ¼-inch dice
1½ cups flour
1½ teaspoons salt
½ teaspoon pepper
2 pounds stew veal, cut into 2-inch chunks
1 bay leaf
½ teaspoon thyme
4 cups water
3 medium onions, cut into wedges
3 medium white turnips (about 1 pound),
    peeled and cut into 1-inch cubes

6 small red potatoes, peeled and cut into
    1-inch cubes
3 medium carrots, cut into 1-inch lengths
1½ teaspoons baking powder
⅓ cup chilled butter, cut into pieces
2 tablespoons light cream or half-and-half
2 medium all-purpose potatoes, peeled, boiled,
    and mashed
2 small zucchini, quartered lengthwise and
    cut into 1-inch pieces
2 tablespoons chopped parsley, for garnish

1. In a Dutch oven or flameproof casserole, sauté the salt pork over medium-high heat until crisp, 10 to 15 minutes. Reserving the fat in the pan, remove the salt pork and set aside.

2. In a shallow bowl, combine ½ cup of the flour with 1 teaspoon of the salt and the pepper. Dredge the veal in the seasoned flour, tapping off any excess.

3. In the rendered pork fat, sauté the veal over medium-high heat, in batches if necessary, until browned on all sides, 7 to 10 minutes.

4. Add the bay leaf, thyme, and water, and bring to a boil. Reduce the heat to medium-low, cover, and simmer until the meat is tender, about 1 hour.

5. Add the onions, turnips, cubed potatoes, and carrots. Increase the heat to medium-high and return to a boil. Reduce the heat to medium-low, cover, and simmer until the vegetables are tender, about 15 minutes.

6. Meanwhile, make the dumplings: In a bowl, combine the remaining 1 cup flour with the baking powder and the remaining ½ teaspoon salt. Cut in the butter until the mixture resembles coarse meal. Stir in the cream and mashed potatoes, and blend to form a soft dough.

7. Increase the heat to medium-high and bring the stew to a boil. Add the zucchini. Drop in the dumpling dough by the tablespoon and boil until the dumplings are cooked through, 5 to 10 minutes, gently stirring.

8. Remove the bay leaf and sprinkle the stew with the parsley and reserved salt pork. Serve hot.   *8 servings*

Pine Bark Stew

Explanations for the curious name of this fish stew from South Carolina are colorful, if not particularly believable. One theory suggests that the stew was always made with freshly caught fish and cooked right at river's edge in a cauldron set over a pine bark fire; another, that the stew was often served on pine bark; a third, that the stew is the color of pine bark; and yet another, that during the American Revolution, when seasonings were hard to come by, the stew was flavored with the small, tender roots of the pine tree.

The fish traditionally used in this stew—catfish, bass, and sheepshead, for example—are native to South Carolina's Pee Dee River, but any firm-fleshed white fish will do. Be sure not to leave out the ketchup; it adds a spicy flavor and is an essential part of the dish. The creators of the stew, of course, would probably have made it with homemade ketchup.

¼ pound bacon (4 to 6 slices)
1 medium onion, chopped (about 1¼ cups)
6 medium plum tomatoes, coarsely chopped
   (about 3½ cups)
2 tablespoons ketchup
1 teaspoon Worcestershire sauce
1 tablespoon sugar
2 teaspoons chili powder

Pinch of cayenne pepper
½ cup canned chicken broth
8 medium boiling potatoes, peeled and sliced
   (about 1 pound)
1½ pounds tilefish fillet, or other firm-fleshed
   white fish, cut into 2-inch-square pieces
¼ cup chopped parsley, for garnish

1. In a Dutch oven or flameproof casserole, cook the bacon over medium heat until crisp, about 10 minutes. Reserving the fat in the pan, drain the bacon on paper towels; crumble and set aside.

2. Add the onion to the bacon fat and sauté over medium heat until the onion is softened but not browned, about 10 minutes.

3. Add the tomatoes, ketchup, Worcestershire sauce, sugar, chili powder, and cayenne, and bring to a boil. Reduce the heat to medium-low, cover, and simmer until the tomatoes fall apart, 10 to 15 minutes.

4. Add the chicken broth. Increase the heat to medium-high and bring to a boil. Add the potatoes, reduce the heat to medium-low, cover, and simmer, stirring occasionally, until the potatoes are just tender, 5 to 8 minutes.

5. Add the fish and simmer, gently stirring, until the fish is opaque, about 5 minutes longer.

6. Serve hot, garnished with the bacon and parsley. *6 servings*

Pine Bark Stew

Kentucky Burgoo

Burgoo is the granddaddy of country stews. In its home state of Kentucky, it is one of the mainstays of Derby Day and is traditionally cooked, in quantities no smaller than five gallons, in large kettles set over outdoor fires. The ingredients vary with the cook, but to be an authentic Kentucky burgoo, the stew must contain mutton (now usually replaced by lamb). Ordinarily this good, old-fashioned stew cooks for seven or eight hours and is typically quite thick. In the recipe below, the cooking time is cut slightly for a somewhat lighter stew.

1½ pounds skinless, boneless chicken breast
1½ pounds boneless beef shank
1 pound stew lamb
6 cups water
1 teaspoon salt
¼ teaspoon black pepper
4 cups shredded cabbage (about ½ pound)
3 medium all-purpose potatoes, peeled and cut into ½-inch cubes (about 3 cups)
3 medium tomatoes, coarsely chopped (about 3 cups), or 1 can (28 ounces) whole tomatoes, drained and chopped
4 medium carrots, diced (about 2 cups)
2 cups fresh okra, or 1 package (10 ounces) frozen

1½ cups corn kernels, fresh (about 3 ears) or frozen
1 medium onion, chopped (about 1¼ cups)
1 large green bell pepper, diced (about 1½ cups)
2 cloves garlic, minced
1½ teaspoons sage
1½ teaspoons thyme
1 bay leaf
5 drops of hot pepper sauce
⅛ teaspoon cayenne pepper
½ pound ham, cut into bite-size pieces
1 cup chopped parsley

1. In a large Dutch oven or flameproof casserole, combine the chicken, beef, lamb, water, salt, and black pepper. Bring to a boil over high heat, skimming any foam that rises to the surface. Reduce the heat to medium-low and simmer, partially covered, until the chicken is tender, 30 to 40 minutes.

2. Remove the chicken to a plate and cover loosely with foil. Continue to simmer the meats, partially covered, until they are tender, about 1½ hours longer. Add the meats to the chicken and keep covered.

3. Add the cabbage, potatoes, tomatoes, carrots, okra, corn, onion, bell pepper, garlic, sage, thyme, bay leaf, hot pepper sauce, and cayenne to the stock in the Dutch oven. Increase the heat to high and bring to a boil. Reduce the heat to medium-low and simmer, uncovered, for 30 minutes.

4. Cut the chicken, beef, and lamb into bite-size pieces and add them and the ham to the Dutch oven. Continue simmering until the meat is heated through, 5 to 10 minutes.

5. Discard the bay leaf. Stir in the parsley and serve hot.   *10 to 12 servings*

CAST-IRON COOKWARE

Iron, perhaps the oldest cooking medium on earth, remains one of the best. Until the mid-19th century, most Americans cooked on the open hearth or used both the hearth and a cast-iron stove. In those days, cast iron was also the only practical and readily available material for pots and pans. Many traditional American recipes, for such dishes as baked beans, griddle cakes, and fried chicken, took advantage of the fine heat-conducting properties of this metal. Today, despite the availability of other types of cookware, many cooks will use only cast iron to prepare such dishes.

Because cast iron absorbs heat slowly and evenly, then retains it, it is ideal for dishes like stews and soups, which improve with slow cooking. It is also good for baking, high-heat searing, and frying. Corn sticks or muffins baked in cast iron will have a crackling crisp crust; chicken seems to brown better in a cast-iron frying pan. Today many types of cast-iron pots and pans are available, including skillets, Dutch ovens, popover and corn-stick pans, bean pots, and kettles.

Part of the appeal of cast iron is its durability; indeed, some pans have been passed down for generations. Properly seasoned and cared for, a cast-iron pan will improve with each use, building up a virtually non-stick surface. To season a new cast-iron pan or to recondition an old one, lightly rub it inside and out with vegetable shortening (not vegetable oil), then place the pan in a 250° oven for two hours. For best results, repeat this process several times before using the pan.

Consider the following guidelines when cooking with cast iron. For baking, it is best to preheat the pan as the oven preheats, then brush the pan with shortening and spoon in the batter. Remember that cast iron is reactive and can cause certain acidic foods like tomatoes to discolor or taste metallic. As a rule, do not use cast iron when cooking with wine, or for making sauces with egg yolks.

To clean cast iron, simply wipe the pan with a paper towel, or if food is stuck on, sprinkle the pan with coarse salt, then rub with a stiff brush. A seasoned pan can be rinsed with soap and water then dried immediately over low heat.

Chicken and Sausage Gumbo

Chicken and Sausage Gumbo

There are dozens of variations on this Louisiana classic, but all gumbos are ladled over white rice and served in soup bowls. For added zest, pass hot sauce on the side.

½ cup flour

1 teaspoon paprika

1 teaspoon salt

½ teaspoon black pepper

¼ teaspoon cayenne pepper

2½ pounds chicken parts, rinsed and
   patted dry

About 3 tablespoons vegetable oil

2 medium onions, chopped (about 2½ cups)

3 cloves garlic, minced

2 stalks celery, chopped (about 1 cup)

1 teaspoon thyme

1 bay leaf

1 teaspoon Worcestershire sauce

5 cups canned chicken broth

½ pound kielbasa, or other garlic sausage, cut
   into ½-inch rounds

2 packages (10 ounces each) frozen okra

1 medium yellow or green bell pepper, cut into
   1-inch squares (about 1 cup)

Steamed rice

2 tablespoons chopped parsley, for garnish

1. In a bowl, combine the flour, paprika, salt, black pepper, and cayenne. Dredge the chicken in the seasoned flour. Shake off any excess and reserve the dredging flour.

2. In a Dutch oven or heavy flameproof casserole, heat 3 tablespoons of the oil over medium-high heat until it is hot and almost smoking. Add the chicken, skin-side down, and cook until golden brown, 2 to 3 minutes per side. Drain the chicken on paper towels.

3. Pour off all but 3 tablespoons of fat (or, if there isn't enough fat, add vegetable oil to come up to 3 tablespoons). Heat the fat and oil over medium-high heat. Add the onions and garlic, and sauté, stirring frequently, until the onions begin to brown, about 5 minutes.

4. Add the reserved dredging flour and continue to cook, stirring constantly, until the flour turns dark brown (but is not burned), 2 to 3 minutes.

5. Add the celery, thyme, bay leaf, Worcestershire sauce, chicken broth, and kielbasa. Increase the heat to high and bring to a boil, stirring frequently.

6. Add the chicken, reduce the heat to medium-low, cover, and simmer until the chicken is tender, about 40 minutes.

7. Remove the chicken and, when it is cool enough to handle, remove the meat from the bones. Cut the meat into cubes and return it to the gumbo.

8. Add the okra and bell pepper. Increase the heat to medium-high, bring the gumbo to a boil, and cook for 5 minutes. Discard the bay leaf.

9. To serve, mound rice in big soup bowls, ladle some gumbo over the rice, and garnish with the parsley. *6 servings*

Cheddar and Broccoli Strata

A strata is in essence a savory bread pudding that is usually flavored with cheese. In this recipe, broccoli is added for color, texture, and a hint of sweetness.

10 slices firm-textured white bread, crusts
    trimmed and bread cut into cubes (about
    5 cups)
3 cups broccoli florets and stems (from about
    2 medium stalks)
2 cups grated extra-sharp Cheddar cheese
    (about ½ pound)

5 eggs, beaten
2½ cups milk
1 teaspoon Worcestershire sauce
½ teaspoon dry mustard
½ teaspoon salt
1 medium onion, chopped (about 1¼ cups)
¼ pound bacon (4 to 6 slices)

1. Butter a 9 x 13-inch baking dish.
2. Spread half of the bread cubes on the bottom of the prepared baking dish. Alternate layers of broccoli, cheese, and bread, ending with cheese.
3. In a bowl, combine the eggs, milk, Worcestershire sauce, mustard, salt, and onion. Pour the mixture over the ingredients in the baking dish. Cover and refrigerate for 6 hours or overnight.
4. Preheat the oven to 350°.
5. Bake the strata, uncovered, for 1 hour, or until a knife inserted in the center comes out clean. Let stand 10 minutes before cutting.
6. Meanwhile, in a large skillet, cook the bacon over medium heat until crisp, about 10 minutes. Drain on paper towels and crumble.
7. Serve the strata topped with the crumbled bacon. *6 to 8 servings*

Fresh Tuna Casserole

Tuna casserole made with fresh tuna steak, red peppers, and scallions is far superior to the school cafeteria concoction most people grew up with.

½ pound tuna steak, about ¾ inch thick
6 ounces egg noodles
1 stick (4 ounces) butter
½ pound mushrooms, coarsely chopped
1 cup chopped scallions (about 5 medium)
1 medium red bell pepper, cut into ½-inch
    squares

3 cloves garlic, minced
¼ cup flour
¾ cup milk
½ cup canned chicken broth
2 cups grated Swiss cheese (about ½ pound)
¼ cup chopped parsley
2 tablespoons grated Parmesan cheese

1. Preheat the broiler.
2. Place the tuna on a foil-lined baking sheet and broil 4 or 5 inches from the heat, 3 to 4 minutes per side, until the flesh is opaque throughout. Let the tuna cool slightly, then flake it with a fork, cover, and set aside.

3. Preheat the oven to 375°. Butter a 1½-quart baking dish.

4. In a large saucepan of boiling salted water, cook the noodles according to the package directions until tender but still firm. Drain, toss with 3 tablespoons of the butter, and set aside.

5. In a medium saucepan, melt the remaining 5 tablespoons butter over medium heat. Add the mushrooms, scallions, red pepper, and garlic, and sauté until the scallions are softened but not browned, about 5 minutes.

6. Sprinkle on the flour and stir to form a paste. Gradually add the milk and chicken broth, and continue cooking, stirring, until thickened, 2 to 3 minutes. Add the Swiss cheese and stir until completely melted. Stir in the parsley, reserved noodles, and tuna.

7. Pour the mixture into the prepared baking dish. Top with the Parmesan and bake for 30 minutes, or until bubbling and golden brown. Serve hot.   *6 servings*

Bowl of Red

Bowl of red is what Texans call chili con carne. It gets its name, and color, from dried red chilies—not from tomatoes, which purists often omit altogether.

¼ cup vegetable oil

1 medium red onion, chopped (about 1½ cups)

3 cloves garlic, minced

2½ pounds beef chuck, cut into ½-inch cubes

⅓ cup chili powder

1 tablespoon ground cumin

2 teaspoons oregano

1 teaspoon paprika

1 can (28 ounces) crushed tomatoes, with their juice

2 cups canned beef broth

1 teaspoon salt

⅓ cup yellow cornmeal

¼ cup water

2 cans (15 ounces each) pinto beans, drained and rinsed

1 cup chopped scallions (about 5 medium)

1. In a Dutch oven or flameproof casserole, heat the oil over medium heat. Add the onion and garlic, and sauté until the onion is softened but not browned, about 10 minutes.

2. Increase the heat to medium-high, add the beef, and sauté until lightly cooked, about 10 minutes.

3. Stir in the chili powder, cumin, oregano, and paprika. Add the tomatoes with their juice, the beef broth, and salt. Bring to a boil, reduce the heat to medium-low, and simmer, covered, until the beef is tender, about 1½ hours.

4. Fifteen minutes before serving, combine the cornmeal and water. Bring the chili back to a boil over medium heat and stir in the cornmeal mixture and the pinto beans. Reduce the heat to medium-low, cover, and simmer, stirring occasionally, until the beans are heated through and the sauce thickens, about 5 minutes.

5. Serve hot, sprinkled with the scallions.   *8 servings*

Brunswick Stew

Brunswick stew is named for Brunswick County, Virginia, where it was first served, so the story goes, at a political rally in 1828. Originally made with squirrel instead of chicken, it is still a favorite at large gatherings, political or otherwise.

1 tablespoon peanut oil
2½ pounds chicken parts, rinsed and patted dry
2 pounds smoked ham hocks
1 can (14 ounces) whole tomatoes, with
   their juice
3 medium fresh plum tomatoes, chopped
2 medium all-purpose potatoes, peeled
   and cut into 1-inch cubes

2 medium onions, cut into wedges
8 cups shredded cabbage (about ½
   medium head)
1 package (10 ounces) frozen lima beans
1½ cups corn kernels, fresh (about 3
   ears) or frozen
2 medium green bell peppers, cut into
   1-inch squares

1. In a Dutch oven or flameproof casserole, heat the oil over medium-high heat. Add the chicken and sauté until browned, about 5 minutes per side.
2. Add the ham hocks, canned and fresh tomatoes, and enough water (about 3 cups) so the liquid just covers the ingredients. Bring to a boil. Reduce the heat, cover, and simmer until the chicken is tender, about 30 minutes.

Brunswick Stew

3. With a slotted spoon, remove the chicken and set aside. Re-cover the stew and simmer for 1 hour longer. Meanwhile, when the chicken is cool enough to handle, remove the meat from the bone. Cover loosely with foil and set aside.

4. Add the potatoes, onions, and cabbage to the stew. Increase the heat to medium-high and bring to a boil. Reduce the heat to medium-low, cover, and simmer until the potatoes are tender, 10 to 15 minutes.

5. Add the lima beans, corn, and green peppers, and cook 10 minutes longer.

6. Remove the ham hocks from the stew and when they are cool enough to handle, cut the meat from the bones. Cut the ham and reserved chicken into 1-inch pieces and return the meat to the stew. Cook, uncovered, until heated through, about 10 minutes. Serve hot. *8 to 10 servings*

Ham and Seafood Jambalaya

Jambalaya, like its cousin paella, often contains a mixture of meat and seafood. This adaptation of the Cajun-Creole classic uses ham, oysters, and shrimp.

2 cups water
1 cup raw short-grain rice
2 tablespoons vegetable oil
2 medium onions, chopped (about 2½ cups)
3 cloves garlic, minced
1 can (35 ounces) whole tomatoes, with their
*   juice*
2 stalks celery, chopped (about 1 cup)
1 medium green bell pepper, diced (about 1 cup)
¼ cup chopped parsley

½ teaspoon hot pepper sauce
1 teaspoon thyme
⅛ teaspoon cayenne pepper
1 bay leaf
1 teaspoon salt
½ teaspoon black pepper
½ pound ham, cut into ½-inch cubes
1 pint shucked oysters, drained
1 pound medium shrimp, shelled and
*   deveined*

1. In a medium saucepan, bring the water to a boil. Add the rice. Reduce the heat to low, cover, and simmer until the rice is tender, about 20 minutes. Fluff the rice with a fork, cover, and set aside.

2. In a Dutch oven or flameproof casserole, heat the oil over medium heat. Add the onions and garlic, and sauté until the onions are softened but not browned, about 10 minutes. Add the tomatoes with their juice, breaking the tomatoes up with a spoon, and simmer for 5 minutes.

3. Add the celery, bell pepper, 2 tablespoons of the parsley, the hot pepper sauce, thyme, cayenne, bay leaf, salt, and black pepper. Cook, stirring frequently, until the vegetables are tender, 25 to 30 minutes.

4. Add the ham and oysters, and cook, stirring, for 5 minutes. Add the shrimp and cook until they just turn pink, 3 to 4 minutes.

5. Add the rice and cook, stirring, until the jambalaya is heated through and the rice has absorbed any liquid in the pan. Discard the bay leaf.

6. Garnish with the remaining 2 tablespoons parsley and serve. *8 servings*

One popular (though doubtful) explanation for the name jambalaya goes thus: One night a gentleman stopped by a New Orleans inn to find nothing left for supper. The owner told the cook, whose name was Jean, to "mix some things together"—balayez in Cajun dialect. The guest loved the dish and named it "Jean Balayez."

Herb and Spice Glossary

◆ *allspice* Pea-size fruit of an evergreen tree grown primarily in Jamaica. Picked just before ripe, then sun-dried, the berry tastes like a mixture of cinnamon, nutmeg, and cloves, hence its name. Use whole for pickling, in gravies, and in seafood dishes. Use ground in fruit preserves, puddings, and baked goods.

allspice

◆ *balm* Flowering plant, also called lemon balm for its citrus fragrance. Bees find balm inviting; in fact, the genus name for balm, *melissa*, is derived from the Latin for honey. Use the young leaves fresh or dried in fruit and vegetable salads. Because heat dissipates the lemon scent, add balm to hot dishes near the end of the cooking time.

◆ *basil* Leafy, aromatic member of the mint family, whose name means "king" in Greek. Basil leaves have been used not only to entice lovers but also to ward off flies. Sweet basil is the most common variety, but more than 150 varieties exist, including lemon, purple, and opal basil. Use fresh in salads, fresh or dried in tomato and egg dishes, and with chicken, lamb, pork,

veal, fish, and shellfish. Avoid powdered basil, which has little flavor.

◆ *bay leaf* Also known as sweet bay or bay laurel, from an evergreen tree or shrub native to the Mediterranean. Wreaths fashioned from the leathery leaves have long been a symbol of honor. Use fresh or dried—judiciously—to add flavor to stocks, soups, stews, sauces, gumbos, pâtés, pickling mixtures, rice puddings, and custards. Always be sure to remove bay leaves before serving any dish.

◆ *caraway seed* Fruit of the caraway plant and member of the parsley family closely related to fennel and dill. Caraway has a taste resembling that of anise. Once thought to chase away evil spirits, the black crescent-shaped seeds are now used to season rye breads, coleslaw, sauerkraut and boiled cabbage, beef stews, and fish and fowl dishes.

cayenne pepper

◆ *cayenne pepper* The red pod of various capsicum hot pepper plants, whole, crushed, or ground. The fiery taste of cayenne is indispensable in chili, and in Creole and Cajun dishes. Used sparingly, cayenne can perk up

soups, sauces, fish, meat, omelets, fowl, and cheese and vegetable dishes.

coriander seed

◆ *coriander seed* Fruit of the coriander plant. The dried seed has a spicy taste suggesting a combination of caraway and cumin, and a sweet smell reminiscent of orange. Use whole or ground, in curries, sausages, lentil and pea soups, gingerbread, and pumpkin pie. (The leaves of the coriander plant, which is also known as cilantro or Chinese parsley, can be used for seasoning as well.)

◆ *cumin seed* Fruit of a plant from the parsley family. Cumin is an ancient spice that was used to pay tithes in biblical times. Its taste is similar to but more bitter than caraway. Used whole or ground it adds to the flavor of curries and chilies, and also enlivens sausages, pickles, chutneys, carrot salads, and breads.

◆ *juniper berry* Fruit of an evergreen shrub of the same name. Juniper berries give gin its distinctive flavor, and tend to impart a resinous taste to whatever food they season. The fleshy pea-like berries are an excellent accompaniment to lamb, squab, pork, duck, rabbit, sauerkraut, and pâtés. Use ground in quiche and tart crusts.

◆ *mace* Lacy, crimson membrane that envelops the growing nutmeg fruit, usually imported from the West Indies or Asia. The flavor of mace is similar to that of nutmeg but more pungent. It is possible to buy this spice in "blades" about an inch long, but it is more commonly sold ground. Use in seafood dishes, fruit salads and sauces, cherry pie, yellow cakes, chocolate dishes, meat stuffings, and with carrots.

mace

◆ *marjoram* Member of the mint family, also called sweet marjoram. An ancient herb, marjoram was used to make beer before the discovery of hops. Fresh or dried, this slightly bitter herb adds interest to soups, tomato sauces, poultry, and meat loaf.

◆ *oregano* From the Greek *oros* and *ganos*, meaning "joy of the mountain." Also known as wild marjoram, oregano is spicier than sweet marjoram, with hints of clove and balsam. Use the leaves fresh or dried to season tomato sauce, pizza, soups, stews, fish, and vegetables.

rosemary

◆ *rosemary* Needle-like leaves of the evergreen shrub of the same name. Used fresh or dried, the leaves have a taste that has been described as a combination of fir, balsam, and ocean air. Used whole, cut with scissors, or crumbled, rosemary adds savor to lamb, pork, veal, and broiled fish. Avoid ground rosemary, as it can give a bitter taste to some foods.

◆ *sage* Delicate and aromatic leaves of an evergreen shrub. The botanical name for sage, *Salvia officinalis*, means to save or heal, and for centuries the herb has been touted as a cure-all. The silvery green, felted leaves can be used fresh, but are generally dried and crumbled (ground sage loses its flavor quickly). Sage is a traditional addition to sausages and stuffings, and also goes well with baked fish and in salad dressings and chowders.

◆ *savory, summer and winter* Closely related plants from the mint family, the winter variety having a slightly harsher flavor than summer savory. Rubbing fresh crushed savory leaves on bee stings helps to ease the pain. In the kitchen, use the leaves fresh or dried to enhance pea soup, barbecue

sauce, green salads, meat pies, and any bean dish.

◆ *tarragon* Flowering herb with a flavor reminiscent of anise. Tarragon is considered essential in *fines herbes* mixtures, and is often used to flavor wine vinegars and mustards. Delicious fresh or dried in consommés and béarnaise sauce, and with lamb, veal, pork, salmon, shellfish, chicken, and tomatoes.

◆ *thyme* Strongly aromatic leaves of an evergreen shrub from the mint family. In Renaissance England, thyme was one of the chief "strewing herbs," used along with lavender and rosemary to banish bad odors. For cooking, use the leaves fresh or dried in chowders, in tomato sauces, and with meat, eggs, and vegetables.

turmeric

◆ *turmeric* Root of a plant from the ginger family. Powdered turmeric has only a slight smell, but imparts the hot spicy taste associated with ginger. It gives a yellow color to curries, mustards, and other foods. Use the dry powder sparingly in chicken, shellfish, lamb, and potato dishes, and to color deviled eggs.

Posole

In the Southwest, posole—or pork and hominy stew—is a feast-day dish traditionally served on Christmas Eve, New Year's Eve, or New Year's Day. Like many regional American stews, posole is made in vast quantities. Although the recipe here serves eight, it can be easily expanded, and the stew freezes exceptionally well. In addition to the lime wedges and vegetable garnishes, serve the posole with a stack of hot corn tortillas, sweet butter, and pitchers of beer.

2 pounds pork shoulder

3½ cups canned beef broth

3 cups water

2 medium onions, 1 sliced and 1 chopped

5 cloves garlic, 2 whole and 3 minced

¾ teaspoon oregano

½ teaspoon salt

2 tablespoons olive oil

2 tablespoons chili powder

2 cans (16 ounces each) hominy, drained

3 medium tomatoes, chopped (about 3 cups), or 1 can (28 ounces) whole tomatoes, drained and chopped

1 can (4 ounces) chopped mild green chilies, drained

1 cup chopped fresh coriander (optional)

1 medium yellow or green bell pepper, cut into ½-inch squares

4 cups shredded lettuce, for garnish

10 radishes, sliced, for garnish

2 limes, cut into wedges, for garnish

1 avocado, diced and sprinkled with lime juice, for garnish

1. In a large saucepan, bring the pork, beef broth, water, the sliced onion, the 2 whole cloves of garlic, the oregano, and salt to a boil over medium-high heat. Reduce the heat to medium-low, cover, and simmer for 2 hours.

2. Reserving the meat but discarding the vegetables, strain the broth through a colander lined with a double thickness of dampened cheesecloth. Skim the fat from the broth, or refrigerate until the fat hardens and then skim. Set the broth aside. Cut the pork into ½-inch cubes.

3. In a Dutch oven or flameproof casserole, heat the olive oil over medium heat. Add the chopped onion and minced garlic, and sauté until the onion is softened but not browned, about 10 minutes. Add the cubed pork and chili powder, and sauté for 1 or 2 minutes longer.

4. Add the reserved pork broth, hominy, tomatoes, green chilies, and coriander (if using). Reduce the heat to medium-low, cover, and simmer for 20 minutes.

5. Add the bell pepper and simmer for 15 minutes longer.

6. Serve the posole with the garnishes on the side.   *8 servings*

Posole

New Mexico Green Chili

What chili con carne is to Texas (see Bowl of Red, page 77), *chile verde* is to New Mexico. In this version of chili, beef is replaced by lamb or pork, red chilies by green chilies (both mild and fiery hot), and beans by potatoes. Wheat flour tortillas make an ideal accompaniment to this spicy stew.

3 tablespoons peanut oil
2 pounds pork shoulder, cut into ½-inch
   cubes
2 stalks celery, chopped (about 1 cup)
3 cans (4 ounces each) chopped mild green
   chilies, drained
3 medium tomatoes, chopped (about 3 cups)
3 cloves garlic, minced
1 fresh jalapeño pepper, seeded and minced
   (see Note, page 43)

4 cups canned chicken broth
2 medium all-purpose potatoes (about 1
   pound), peeled and cut into ½-inch cubes
1 medium green bell pepper, diced (about 1
   cup)
1 medium red bell pepper, diced (about 1 cup)
1 cup sour cream, for garnish
¼ cup chopped fresh coriander, for garnish

1. In a Dutch oven or flameproof casserole, heat the oil over medium-high heat. Add the pork, in batches if necessary, and sauté until browned, 5 to 10 minutes.

2. Add the celery, mild green chilies, tomatoes, garlic, jalapeño, and chicken broth. Reduce the heat to medium-low, cover, and simmer until the meat is tender, about 1 hour.

3. Add the potatoes and cook another 30 minutes.

4. Five minutes before serving, add the green and red bell peppers to heat through.

5. Serve the chili hot, topped with sour cream and fresh coriander.   *8 servings*

Red Snapper Muddle

A muddle is a thick fish stew native to the Outer Banks of North Carolina and nearby eastern Virginia. Local cooks make their muddles with rockfish, a mid-Atlantic colloquialism for striped bass. If you cannot get striped bass, use a full-flavored, firm-fleshed white fish, such as the red snapper called for in this recipe. Other equally good choices include tilefish, scrod, or butterfish.

¼ pound bacon (4 to 6 slices)
1 medium red onion, sliced (about 1½ cups)
1 cup chopped scallions (about 5 medium)
1 can (14 ounces) whole tomatoes, with
   their juice
6 small red potatoes (about 1 pound), peeled
   and thinly sliced

½ teaspoon salt
¼ teaspoon pepper
1 pound red snapper fillet, cut into
   1-inch squares
4 eggs
2 tablespoons chopped fresh coriander,
   for garnish

1. In a Dutch oven or flameproof casserole, cook the bacon over medium heat until crisp, about 10 minutes. Reserving the fat in the pan, drain the bacon on paper towels; crumble and set aside.

2. To the bacon fat, add the onion and scallions and sauté over medium heat, stirring, for 2 minutes. Add the tomatoes with their juice, breaking the tomatoes up with a spoon, and cook for 2 minutes longer.

3. Add the potatoes, salt, and pepper. Reduce the heat to medium-low, cover, and simmer until the potatoes are tender, 15 to 20 minutes.

4. Add the fish, cover, and simmer for 1 minute longer.

5. One at a time, break an egg into a saucer and carefully slide it on top of the simmering stew. Cover and simmer, basting the eggs occasionally with some of the liquid, until the eggs are poached, 3 to 4 minutes.

6. To serve, spoon some of the stew into a soup bowl and top with a poached egg, some crumbled bacon, and fresh coriander.

4 servings

American Lamb Stew

Lamb stew seems to cut across a number of regional and ethnic boundaries. Although the seasonings may vary, most recipes seem to include potatoes, onions, and carrots. In this stew, lima beans are added to the vegetable mix, and rosemary is used to heighten the flavors of the meat.

½ cup flour
1 teaspoon salt
½ teaspoon pepper
2½ pounds stew lamb, cut into 2-inch chunks
About 3 tablespoons vegetable oil
1½ cups dry red wine
1½ cups canned beef broth
10 shallots (about ½ pound), or 5 small white
  onions, peeled and left whole

3 cloves garlic, minced
1 to 2 teaspoons rosemary, crumbled
5 medium boiling potatoes, peeled and
  quartered
6 medium carrots, cut into 2-inch lengths
1 package (10 ounces) frozen lima beans
¼ cup chopped parsley, for garnish

1. In a shallow bowl, combine the flour, salt, and pepper. Dredge the lamb in the seasoned flour, tapping off the excess.

2. In a Dutch oven or flameproof casserole, heat 2 tablespoons of the oil over medium-high heat. In two batches, add the lamb and brown evenly, 7 to 10 minutes, adding the remaining 1 tablespoon oil with the second batch (use more oil if necessary to prevent sticking).

3. Add the red wine, beef broth, shallots, garlic, and rosemary. Reduce the heat to medium-low, cover, and simmer until the meat is almost tender, about 30 minutes.

4. Add the potatoes and carrots, and cook another 25 minutes.

5. Add the lima beans and simmer until heated through, about 5 minutes. Serve hot, garnished with the parsley.

8 servings

FOUR

Vegetables and Salads

*colorful, flavorful additions
to country meals*

Country-style recipes for vegetables and salads were relatively scarce in early American cookbooks, perhaps because, in the days before refrigeration, produce had to be prepared soon after it was taken from the garden and was served up simply, with little seasoning or sauce. "Receipts" consequently were not often kept for such dishes. Moreover, once the growing season was past, most vegetables were gone until the following year unless a housewife canned or dried them.

One recipe in this chapter, however, can be traced back to an actual recipe from the New England colonies: succotash. In fact, it was the Indians who taught the colonists to grow corn and beans, and to combine them in this simple dish. Many of the other recipes in the chapter are regional and ethnic specialties that came into existence later, as the country was settled. It is these recipes—for Shaker Green Beans, Pennsylvania-German Fried Tomatoes, and Vidalia Onion Pie—that have become synonymous with country-style vegetable and salad cookery today.

A melange of country vegetables ready for side dishes and salads.

Succotash with Sweet Red Pepper

Succotash—from the Narraganset Indian word *misickquatash*—was one of the first dishes the Pilgrims learned to make with New World ingredients. Always based on corn and lima beans (fresh today, but usually dried in colonial days), this recipe includes green beans and red pepper for contrasting color and texture.

5 tablespoons butter
½ pound green beans, cut into 2-inch lengths
2 cups corn kernels, fresh (about 4 ears) or
  frozen
1 package (10 ounces) frozen lima beans

1 small red bell pepper, diced (about ½ cup)
1 cup chopped scallions (about 5 medium)
½ teaspoon salt
¼ teaspoon black pepper
½ cup heavy cream

1. In a medium saucepan, melt the butter over medium-high heat. Add the green beans, corn, lima beans, bell pepper, scallions, salt, and black pepper, and stir-fry for 5 minutes.

2. Add the cream, reduce the heat to medium-low, cover, and simmer, stirring occasionally, for 20 minutes.

4 to 6 servings

During colonial times, Indian women dried corn and beans in preparation for lean winters. Often these ingredients were made into succotash, which could be frozen in the snow. When it was time for a meal, chunks of frozen succotash were hacked off with a tomahawk, then reheated over a fire.

Hominy Baked with Cream and Cheddar

Hominy is dried corn that has been soaked—usually in a weak solution of lye and water—to remove the kernels' tough outer layers. Originally a staple of the Indian diet in the Northeast, today it is primarily a feature of Southern cooking. In its whole, cooked form (most recipes call for the canned variety), hominy is served as a vegetable side dish. However, hominy that has been coarsely ground is known as grits.

2 cans (16 ounces each) hominy, drained
1 medium green bell pepper, chopped (about 1
  cup)
1 small onion, chopped (about ½ cup)
¼ cup diced canned mild green chilies, drained
1 cup grated white Cheddar cheese (about
  ¼ pound)

1 cup heavy cream
2 eggs, beaten
2 slices firm-textured white bread,
  torn into crumbs
2 tablespoons butter, melted

1. Preheat the oven to 375°. Butter a 1-quart baking dish.

2. In a large bowl, combine the hominy, green pepper, onion, green chilies, Cheddar cheese, cream, and eggs. Turn the mixture into the prepared baking dish.

3. In a small bowl, toss the breadcrumbs with the melted butter. Top the hominy with the buttered crumbs and bake for 25 to 30 minutes, or until the crumb topping is browned.

4 servings

Calabacitas

Calabacitas, a sort of Southwestern succotash, is usually a combination of zucchini and corn, but it can also be made with yellow squash. To give it a New Mexican flavor, add about one-quarter cup diced mild green chilies.

1 tablespoon olive oil

4 tablespoons butter

4 medium zucchini (about 1 pound), halved lengthwise and cut into ½-inch half-rounds

1 medium onion, chopped (about 1¼ cups)

1 medium red bell pepper, cut into thin strips

1 fresh jalapeño pepper, seeded and minced (see Note, page 43)

2 cloves garlic, minced

1 cup corn kernels, fresh (about 2 ears) or frozen, thawed and drained

½ cup heavy cream

½ teaspoon salt

¼ teaspoon black pepper

½ cup grated Cheddar cheese (about 2 ounces)

1. In a large skillet, heat the olive oil and butter over medium-high heat. Add the zucchini, onion, red bell pepper, jalapeño, and garlic, and sauté until the zucchini is softened slightly but not browned, about 5 minutes.

2. Add the corn, cream, salt, and black pepper. Reduce the heat to low, cover, and simmer until the zucchini is still slightly crisp, about 5 minutes.

3. Remove from the heat and stir in the cheese until just melted.   *4 servings*

Calabacitas

Green Corn Pudding

Old cookbooks often refer to corn pudding as green corn pudding because it is made with fresh (green) corn, not dried corn. To get the most out of fresh corn, after you cut the kernels off with a sharp knife, run the blunt edge of the knife over the cut cobs to release more of the sweet corn milk and get the last tender bits of kernel.

3 eggs
1 cup heavy cream
1 cup milk
2 tablespoons flour
2 teaspoons sugar
¼ teaspoon nutmeg

¼ teaspoon salt
⅛ teaspoon cayenne pepper
3 cups corn kernels, fresh (about 6 ears) or
    frozen, thawed and well drained
1½ cups chopped scallions (about 8
    medium)

1. Preheat the oven to 375°. Butter a shallow 1½-quart baking dish.
2. In a large bowl, blend the eggs, cream, and milk. Add the flour, sugar, nutmeg, salt, and cayenne. Stir in the corn and scallions.
3. Turn the mixture into the prepared baking dish. Set the baking dish into a larger pan and place in the oven. Pour enough hot water into the larger pan to come halfway up the sides of the baking dish. Bake the pudding for 1 hour, or until a knife inserted in the center comes out clean.

4 to 6 servings

Cucumber-Onion Salad

Similar in taste and texture to a fresh pickle, this tart-sweet and crunchy salad makes a fine complement to simple roast poultry or grilled meat.

2 medium cucumbers
2 teaspoons salt
⅓ cup cider vinegar
⅓ cup sour cream
3 tablespoons light brown sugar

½ teaspoon Dijon mustard
¼ teaspoon pepper
1 medium red onion, thinly sliced
2 tablespoons chopped parsley, for
    garnish

1. With a vegetable peeler, remove lengthwise strips of cucumber peel to create a striped pattern on the cucumbers.
2. Cut the cucumbers into thin rounds and place in a colander. Sprinkle the cucumber slices with the salt, toss well, and let stand for 15 minutes. Rinse the cucumbers well and pat dry.
3. In a small bowl, whisk together the vinegar, sour cream, brown sugar, mustard, and pepper. Place the cucumbers and sliced onion in a serving bowl, pour the dressing over them, and toss to coat. Refrigerate for at least 2 hours, or until ready to serve.
4. Garnish the salad with the chopped parsley and serve.

4 servings

Yellow Velvet

This rich, buttery corn and summer squash recipe, from the now-defunct Shaker village in Harvard, Massachusetts, more than lives up to its name.

2 cups corn kernels, fresh (about 4 ears) or
    frozen
1 small onion, chopped (about ¾ cup)
½ cup heavy cream
½ teaspoon sugar

3 tablespoons butter
3 medium yellow squash, such as crookneck,
    cut into ½-inch rounds (about 4 cups)
¼ teaspoon salt
¼ teaspoon pepper

1. In a medium saucepan, combine the corn, onion, cream, and sugar. Cover and simmer over medium-low heat until the corn is just tender, about 15 minutes for fresh and 7 to 10 minutes for frozen.

2. Meanwhile, in another medium saucepan, melt the butter over medium heat. Add the squash, salt, and pepper. Cover and cook, stirring occasionally, for 10 minutes.

3. Purée the squash in a food processor or blender. Stir the squash purée into the corn and simmer 5 minutes longer, or until heated through.
    4 servings

Fresh Lime Gelatin Salad

Anyone who has ever had this very American side dish will be surprised at how easy it is to make from scratch. This pale-green salad, made with fresh lime juice and maple syrup, is head and shoulders above the too-sweet and too-green packaged gelatin mixes. As with any molded gelatin salad, you can experiment with other fruit, as long as you do not use fresh pineapple, papaya, kiwi fruit, or figs—which all contain enzymes that prevent gelatin from setting.

2 envelopes unflavored gelatin
½ cup cold water
1½ cups boiling water
½ cup lime juice (about 3 limes)
½ cup maple syrup

4 teaspoons grated lime zest
1 can (11 ounces) mandarin oranges,
    drained
2 small bananas, cut into ¼-inch slices
    (about 1 cup)

1. In a medium bowl, soften the gelatin in the cold water. Add the boiling water and stir to completely dissolve the gelatin.

2. Add the lime juice, maple syrup, and lime zest. Stir well and place in the refrigerator until the gelatin begins to gel slightly, about 30 minutes.

3. Meanwhile, chill a decorative 1-quart mold or bowl.

4. Gently fold the mandarin oranges and bananas into the partially gelled gelatin. Rinse the mold in cold water and pour the gelatin mixture into the mold. Refrigerate the salad until completely set, about 6 hours.
    4 servings

Multi-Bean Salad

This colorful variation on the traditional three-bean salad combines kidney beans, green beans, chickpeas, and lima beans. The recipe serves eight to ten as a side dish, but if you double the ingredients and serve crusty bread or rolls with the salad, it makes a good main course for a summer lunch or light supper.

1 cup dried red kidney beans, rinsed and picked over (see Note)

1 cup dried chickpeas, rinsed and picked over (see Note)

¼ pound fresh green beans, cut into 2-inch lengths

1 package (10 ounces) frozen lima beans, thawed

1 medium yellow bell pepper, cut into 1-inch squares (about 1 cup)

1 medium red bell pepper, cut into 1-inch squares (about 1 cup)

1½ cups chopped scallions (about 8 medium)

2 cloves garlic, minced

½ cup olive oil

½ cup red wine vinegar

2 tablespoons lemon juice

1 tablespoon Dijon mustard

2 teaspoons salt

½ teaspoon black pepper

½ teaspoon sugar

1 head Boston lettuce, separated into leaves

1. In a large saucepan, soak the kidney beans and chickpeas overnight in water to cover by 3 inches. Or place the beans in a large saucepan with water to cover by 2 inches, bring to a boil, and boil for 2 minutes. Remove from the heat, cover, and let stand for 1 hour.

2. Drain the beans, cover with water by 3 inches, and cook until tender, about 2 hours. Drain well.

3. In a saucepan of simmering salted water, blanch the green beans until crisp-tender, about 1 minute. Rinse in cold water, drain, and set aside.

4. Cook the lima beans according to the package directions and drain well.

5. In a large serving bowl, combine the kidney beans, chickpeas, green beans, lima beans, yellow pepper, red pepper, and scallions.

6. In a small bowl, blend the garlic, olive oil, vinegar, lemon juice, mustard, salt, black pepper, and sugar. Pour the dressing over the salad and toss well to combine.

7. Cover and refrigerate the salad for at least 2½ hours (or longer for more flavor), tossing occasionally to coat the vegetables evenly with the dressing.

8. To serve, line individual salad plates with the Boston lettuce leaves and spoon the bean salad on top.   *8 to 10 servings*

NOTE: To save time, you may want to substitute canned beans. For the kidney beans, use 2½ cups canned; for the chickpeas, use 3 cups canned. In both cases, drain and rinse the beans well before using.

Multi-Bean Salad

Vidalia Onion Pie with Bacon and Cheese

Vidalia onions are an exceptionally sweet variety of onion (some devotees insist that they can be eaten out of hand like apples) that are grown in and around the town of Vidalia in southeastern Georgia. Other types of sweet onion—such as Walla Walla and Maui—or red onions can be used instead.

PASTRY
1½ cups flour
¼ teaspoon salt
1 stick (4 ounces) chilled butter, cut into pieces
3 tablespoons sour cream
1 to 2 tablespoons water

FILLING
3 slices bacon
1 pound Vidalia onions, thinly sliced

3 eggs
½ cup milk
½ cup sour cream
1 tablespoon flour
¼ teaspoon nutmeg
⅛ teaspoon pepper
1 cup grated Swiss cheese (about
    ¼ pound)
2 tablespoons chopped parsley,
    for garnish

To keep from crying when cutting an onion, try holding three (no more, no less) matchsticks in your mouth as you chop. More traditional methods include parboiling the onion before peeling, or freezing the onion for half an hour before cutting it.

1. Make the pastry: In a large bowl, combine the flour and salt. With a pastry blender or two knives, cut the butter in until the mixture resembles coarse meal. Blend in the sour cream. Sprinkle on 1 tablespoon of the water and work it into the dough, adding up to 1 more tablespoon of water to form a dough that can be gathered into a ball. Pat the dough into a disc shape, wrap in plastic wrap, and refrigerate for at least 30 minutes.

2. On a lightly floured surface, roll the dough out into a 12-inch circle, then fit it into a 9-inch pie pan. Trim the overhang to an even ½ inch all the way around. Fold the overhang over and crimp the dough to form a decorative border. Prick the bottom of the crust lightly with a fork. Refrigerate the pie shell for 30 minutes.

3. Preheat the oven to 400°. Line the pie shell with foil and fill with dried beans or pie weights. Bake for 8 minutes. Remove the foil and beans, and bake the pastry for 8 to 10 minutes longer, or until lightly golden. Remove the pie shell from the oven and reduce the oven temperature to 375°.

4. Make the filling: In a large skillet, cook the bacon over medium heat until crisp, about 10 minutes. Reserving the fat in the skillet, drain the bacon on paper towels; crumble and set aside.

5. In the bacon fat, sauté the onions over medium heat until softened but not browned, about 10 minutes.

6. Meanwhile, in a medium bowl, whisk together the eggs, milk, sour cream, flour, nutmeg, and pepper.

7. Spread the onions evenly over the bottom of the pie shell. Sprinkle the reserved bacon and the cheese evenly on top. Pour the custard mixture into the pie shell and bake for 20 minutes, or until the custard has set and the top is golden brown.

8. Serve the pie warm, garnished with the parsley.   *4 to 6 servings*

Vidalia Onion Pie with Bacon and Cheese

Texas Caviar

Texas caviar—or marinated black-eyed peas—is a favorite side dish in its namesake state, where it is served as a sort of relish or as a summer salad. Black-eyed peas (also called cowpeas) are grown in Texas, and the natives make an annual display of their fondness for them at the Black-Eyed Pea Jamboree in the town of Athens, Texas, southeast of Dallas.

2 packages (10 ounces each) frozen black-eyed
  peas, thawed
½ cup chopped red onion (about 1 small)
½ cup chopped scallions (2 to 3 medium)
2 tablespoons chopped parsley

½ cup olive oil
¼ cup red wine vinegar
½ teaspoon salt
¼ teaspoon pepper
1 clove garlic, lightly crushed

1. In a large saucepan of boiling salted water, cook the peas until tender, about 10 minutes. Drain well and pat dry with paper towels.

2. Place the black-eyed peas in a bowl and stir in the onion, scallions, and parsley. Add the oil, vinegar, salt, pepper, and garlic and stir well. Refrigerate for at least 2 days and up to 2 weeks. Remove the garlic after 1 day.　　*4 servings*

Louisiana Maque Choux

Maque choux is a Cajun dish whose name remains a mystery: its extremely loose (and highly improbable) translation from the French is mock cabbages. Traditionally, maque choux is corn stewed with tomatoes, peppers, onion, and cayenne—the staple flavorings of Cajun cooking.

¼ pound bacon (4 to 6 slices)
1 large onion, chopped (about 1½ cups)
2 cloves garlic, minced
2 cups corn kernels, fresh (about 4 ears) or
  frozen
2 medium tomatoes, chopped (about 2 cups)

1 large green bell pepper, chopped (about
  1½ cups)
⅓ cup heavy cream
1 teaspoon sugar
½ teaspoon salt
¼ teaspoon cayenne pepper

1. In a Dutch oven or flameproof casserole, cook the bacon over medium heat until crisp, about 10 minutes. Reserving the fat in the pan, drain the bacon on paper towels; crumble and set aside.

2. In the bacon fat, sauté the onion and garlic over medium heat until the onion is softened but not browned, about 10 minutes.

3. Stir in the corn, tomatoes, green pepper, cream, sugar, salt, and cayenne. Increase the heat to medium-high and bring to a boil. Reduce the heat to medium-low and simmer, partially covered, until the corn is tender, about 10 minutes.

4. Serve hot, topped with the crumbled bacon.　　*4 servings*

Peas with Fresh Mint

Thomas Jefferson, who is credited with introducing peas to America, would very likely have served them in the English manner, with fresh mint.

3 pounds fresh peas, shelled (about 3 cups), or
   2 packages (10 ounces each) frozen
¾ cup chopped scallions (about 3 medium)
⅓ cup chopped fresh mint

¾ cup canned chicken broth
1 tablespoon butter
¾ teaspoon sugar

   Place the peas, scallions, mint, chicken broth, butter, and sugar in a medium saucepan. Bring to a boil over medium-high heat. Reduce the heat to medium-low, cover, and cook until the peas are crisp-tender, 3 to 4 minutes.   *4 servings*

Hot German Potato Salad

Hot salad dressing made with vinegar and bacon drippings is a common feature of German-American cooking. It is delicious with most vegetables and salad greens.

12 medium red potatoes (about 2 pounds)
¼ pound bacon (4 to 6 slices)
1 medium red onion, chopped (about 1¼ cups)
3 tablespoons flour
1½ tablespoons sugar
¾ teaspoon dry mustard
¾ teaspoon salt
½ teaspoon celery seed

½ teaspoon black pepper
¾ cup water
⅔ cup cider vinegar
3 hard-cooked eggs, coarsely chopped
1 small green bell pepper, chopped
   (about ¾ cup)
2 stalks celery, chopped (about 1 cup)
¼ cup chopped parsley

   1. In a large saucepan of simmering salted water, cook the potatoes until tender, 30 to 35 minutes. Drain and set aside.

   2. Meanwhile, in a large nonreactive skillet, cook the bacon over medium heat until crisp, about 10 minutes. Reserving the fat, drain the bacon and set aside.

   3. In the bacon fat, sauté the onion over medium heat until softened but not browned, about 10 minutes. Stir in the flour, sugar, mustard, salt, celery seed, and black pepper. Reduce the heat to low and cook, stirring constantly, until the mixture has lightly thickened, about 5 minutes.

   4. Remove the skillet from the heat and stir in the water and vinegar. Bring the dressing to a boil, stirring constantly, and cook for 1 minute. Remove from the heat.

   5. Add the reserved crumbled bacon to the hot dressing. Slice the unpeeled potatoes into the dressing and stir gently to coat them. Return the skillet to medium heat and cook, stirring gently, until the dressing is hot and bubbly, about 1 minute.

   6. Transfer the hot potatoes to a large serving bowl. Stir in the eggs, green pepper, celery, and parsley. Serve the salad warm.   *6 to 8 servings*

pansies

anise hyssop

oregano

nasturtiums

violets

pineapple sage

roses

borage

daisies

lavender

marigolds

EDIBLE FLOWERS

The blossoms of many herbs and ornamental plants are edible and have been used since ancient times with cooked and uncooked foods. Not only do flowers make colorful garnishes for soups, salads, pasta, poultry, and many other dishes, they can add aroma and flavor as well.

Indeed, edible flowers taste much like their scent. Flower blossoms offer a variety of tastes: nasturtiums, for example, are peppery, carnations are spicy, and clover is reminiscent of honey. Herb blossoms, such as those from sage, lavender, and oregano, have a stronger flavor than the stems and leaves of these plants.

Although many types of flowers can be eaten, some, like lily-of-the-valley, iris, sweet pea, and rhododendron, are highly toxic. To ensure that the flowers you plan to eat are safe, buy them from a gourmet shop or by mail order from one of the "boutique" farms specializing in organically grown edible flowers. Never eat flowers from a florist's shop, because these are often treated with chemicals.

For information on foraging for edible flowers or growing your own, consult field guides and garden books dealing with food plants. There are also a number of cookbooks devoted to the subject.

The edible flowers at left are just a sampling of the many types that can enhance your country cooking.

Avocado and Grapefruit Salad with Poppy-Seed Dressing

The bitterness of the endive and grapefruit and the richness of the avocado serve as counterpoints to the sweetness of this poppy-seed dressing.

2 tablespoons distilled white vinegar
2 tablespoons sugar
1/4 teaspoon dry mustard
1/8 teaspoon salt
3 1/2 tablespoons light olive oil
1 tablespoon poppy seeds

24 cherry tomatoes, halved
4 small Belgian endives, cut into 2-inch lengths
2 pink grapefruits, peeled, all white membrane removed, and sectioned
2 small avocados, peeled and cubed
1 cup chopped scallions (about 5 medium)

1. In a small bowl, whisk together the vinegar, sugar, mustard, and salt, until the sugar and salt dissolve.

2. Whisking constantly, add the oil in a slow steady stream until the dressing is thick and smooth. Stir in the poppy seeds.

3. In a large serving bowl, combine the tomatoes, endives, grapefruit sections, avocados, and scallions. Pour the dressing over the salad and toss gently.   *6 servings*

Pennsylvania-German Fried Tomatoes

Pennsylvania-German Fried Tomatoes

Pennsylvania-German cooks tend to treat the tomato as a fruit and not a vegetable, using it more often in pies and compotes than as a savory side dish. When tomatoes are served as a side dish, however, sugar is often added to play up the vegetable's natural sweetness. For a tarter variation, substitute green tomatoes for the red.

1 pound plum tomatoes, cut lengthwise
   into ½-inch slices
⅓ cup flour
1 teaspoon salt
½ teaspoon pepper

4 tablespoons butter
¼ cup (packed) dark brown sugar
½ cup heavy cream
2 tablespoons chopped parsley, for
   garnish

1. Pat the tomato slices dry with paper towels. Place the flour in a shallow bowl.

2. Sprinkle the tomato slices on both sides with the salt and pepper, then dip them in the flour to coat them thoroughly. Tap off any excess.

3. In a large skillet, preferably nonstick (see Note), melt the butter over medium heat. Add the tomato slices, in batches, and cook them until they are lightly browned on the bottom, about 5 minutes.

4. Sprinkle the tomatoes with 2 tablespoons of the sugar and, with a spatula, carefully turn them over. Sprinkle the tomatoes with the remaining 2 tablespoons sugar. Cook the tomatoes until they are golden on the bottom but still hold their shape, about 4 minutes longer. Transfer them to a serving platter.

5. Pour the cream into the skillet, increase the heat to medium-high, and bring it to a boil, stirring constantly. Boil until the sauce thickens, 2 to 3 minutes.

6. To serve, pour the sauce over the tomatoes and garnish with the parsley.

4 servings

NOTE: If you do not use a nonstick pan or a well-seasoned skillet, you may need to use more butter to keep the tomatoes from sticking.

Apple-Glazed Sweet Potatoes with Raisins

There are two types of sweet potato available in this country: one has a pale yellow, slightly dry flesh; the other has a moist, deep orange flesh. The orange-colored sweet potato is often sold as a "yam," which is a misnomer since a true yam is a tropical vegetable rarely seen in American markets. Either type of sweet potato is fine in this recipe.

6 medium sweet potatoes (about 2 pounds)	*2 tablespoons frozen apple juice concentrate*
About 1 stick (4 ounces) butter	*2 tablespoons water*
½ cup (packed) dark brown sugar	*½ cup golden raisins*

1. In a large saucepan of simmering salted water, cook the sweet potatoes until nearly tender, 30 to 35 minutes. Drain, and when cool enough to handle, peel the sweet potatoes, and cut them into ½-inch slices.

2. In a large skillet, melt 4 tablespoons of the butter over medium heat. Add the sweet potato slices and cook until browned on both sides, 10 to 15 minutes. Add up to 4 tablespoons more butter, if necessary, to prevent the slices from sticking.

3. Sprinkle the brown sugar, apple juice concentrate, water, and raisins over the sweet potatoes. Increase the heat to medium-high and cook, shaking the pan occasionally, until the syrup thickens slightly, 2 to 3 minutes. Serve the sweet potatoes with some of the raisins and syrup.

6 servings

The Pennsylvania Germans are famous for the abundance of their dining tables. It is not unusual for twelve separate dishes to be offered at one meal, and often all the dishes are set out at once. Frequently a fruit pie is served both with the main course and as a dessert.

Shaker Green Bean Salad

The Shakers—accomplished herbalists who grew medicinal herbs as cash crops—made extensive use of herbs in their cooking, especially in vegetable and salad recipes. Shaker cooks also cooked with flowers, including pickled nasturtium buds, which would have replaced the capers in the recipe below.

*½ pound green beans, cut into 2-inch
    lengths
¼ cup tarragon vinegar
1 teaspoon Dijon mustard
½ teaspoon tarragon
½ teaspoon salt
¼ teaspoon pepper*

*1 tablespoon capers
2 medium shallots, minced, or 2 tablespoons
    minced onion
1 cup chopped scallions (about 5 medium)
½ cup olive oil
1 head of Bibb lettuce, torn into bite-size
    pieces*

1. In a large saucepan of simmering salted water, cook the beans until crisp-tender, 2 to 3 minutes. Drain, then rinse under cold running water and drain again. Cover the beans and refrigerate until ready to serve.
2. Just before serving, combine the vinegar, mustard, tarragon, salt, pepper, capers, shallots, and scallions in a salad bowl. Gradually whisk in the olive oil.
3. Add the beans and lettuce, and toss the salad gently. *4 servings*

Tart Red and Green Coleslaw

Coleslaw, from the Dutch *kool* (cabbage) and *sla* (salad), has been a feature of American cooking since the 18th century. Over the years, coleslaw has taken many forms: some are quite sweet (and even have pineapple in them), some are made with vinaigrette, some are made with hot dressings and wilted cabbage. This recipe belongs to the crisp cabbage and tart dressing school of coleslaw making.

*6 cups shredded red cabbage (about ½ pound)
6 cups shredded green cabbage (about ½
    pound)
1 small red bell pepper, slivered (about 1 cup)
⅓ cup mayonnaise
½ cup sour cream*

*½ cup plain yogurt
2 tablespoons cider vinegar
1 teaspoon caraway seed
1 teaspoon mustard seed
1 teaspoon salt
¼ teaspoon black pepper*

1. In a large serving bowl, toss together the cabbages and the red bell pepper.
2. In a small bowl, blend the mayonnaise, sour cream, yogurt, vinegar, caraway seed, mustard seed, salt, and black pepper. Pour the dressing over the vegetables and toss well to combine.
3. Serve the coleslaw chilled. *6 to 8 servings*

Beets in Orange-Honey Sauce

Glazing is a traditional way of cooking this earthy-tasting vegetable. In this recipe the beets are glazed with honey, and sour cream is added to round out the flavors.

2½ pounds small to medium beets, trimmed but
   unpeeled
¼ cup sour cream

2 tablespoons butter
2 tablespoons honey
2 teaspoons grated orange zest

   1. In a large saucepan of simmering water, cook the beets, covered, until tender, about 20 minutes. Rinse under cold running water and drain.

   2. Rub the beet skins off, then cut the beets into ¼-inch slices. Return the beets to the saucepan. Stir in the sour cream, butter, honey, and orange zest. Cook the beets over medium heat until warmed through, about 5 minutes.   *4 servings*

Peas and Cheese Salad

Layered salads are a phenomenon born of the potluck supper: some clever potluck-supper-goer developed a salad that benefits from being assembled and dressed the day before it is to be served. There are many variations on the theme, but most layered salads seem to include peas and cheese.

1½ cups mayonnaise
3 tablespoons lemon juice
1 tablespoon Dijon mustard
1 teaspoon sugar
¼ teaspoon black pepper
4 cups shredded Romaine lettuce
5 stalks celery, chopped (about 2½ cups)
4 hard-cooked eggs, thinly sliced

1 package (10 ounces) frozen peas, thawed and
   drained
1 large red bell pepper, chopped (about 1½
   cups)
1 large red onion, thinly sliced
1 cup grated Cheddar cheese (about ¼ pound)
¼ pound bacon (4 to 6 slices)
2 tablespoons chopped parsley, for garnish

   1. In a small bowl, combine the mayonnaise, lemon juice, mustard, sugar, and black pepper.

   2. In a large glass bowl, arrange the lettuce on the bottom, then add successive layers of celery, eggs, peas, red pepper, and onion. Pour the mayonnaise dressing evenly over the top of the salad. Sprinkle the Cheddar on top. Cover and refrigerate for 8 hours, or overnight.

   3. Before serving, cook the bacon in a heavy skillet over medium heat until crisp, about 10 minutes. Drain on paper towels and crumble.

   4. Sprinkle the salad with the crumbled bacon and garnish with the parsley. Either toss the salad before serving, or leave the salad in layers and offer each person a layered portion.   *8 servings*

Rice, Beans, Potatoes, and Grits

staples of the country larder

While rice, beans, potatoes, and grits (coarsely ground dried white corn) have traditionally had a reputation as peasant fare, today they are an essential—and hardly humble—addition to the country dining table.

All of these foods have a long history in country cookery. The American colonists brought rice with them to the New World. While it grew poorly in most regions, rice did very well in the South and eventually became a staple there. Grits were also a Southern favorite, often served instead of rice. Although the Irish first introduced the potato to New England in 1719, it did not become widely eaten in this country until the 19th century. It seems the early settlers much preferred beans to spuds.

This chapter features both traditional and contemporary recipes for rice, beans, potatoes, and grits. All make excellent accompaniments to the main dishes in this book, and some, like Hoppin' John, can be a meal in themselves.

Potatoes, grits, white and wild rice, and a selection of dried legumes.

Sesame-Coated Fried Grits

Grits are coarsely ground dried white corn that is usually boiled and served as a side dish like rice. As in this recipe, grits can also be cooked, cooled until firm, cut into squares, and fried. Serve fried grits as an accompaniment to any meat dish with a sauce or gravy, or for breakfast (omit the scallions and pepper), with maple syrup.

2¼ cups water
2 cups milk
1 teaspoon salt
½ teaspoon pepper
1 cup grits

4 eggs
1 cup chopped scallions (about 5 medium)
2 cups fine fresh breadcrumbs (about 8 slices)
½ cup sesame seeds
7 tablespoons butter

In South Carolina sesame seeds are called benne seeds, from the West African word bene, *meaning sesame plant. One of the earliest uses for these nutty seeds was in the benne wafer, a simple cracker that is still a popular accompaniment for cocktails in Charleston.*

1. In a medium saucepan, bring the water, milk, salt, and pepper to a boil. Gradually stir in the grits. Reduce the heat to medium-low and simmer, uncovered, stirring frequently until thick, about 5 minutes.

2. Lightly beat 2 of the eggs. Remove the saucepan from the heat, then stir the beaten eggs and the scallions into the hot grits. Pour the mixture into an 8-inch square pan, spread it evenly, and chill until firm, about 1 hour.

3. In a shallow bowl, beat the remaining 2 eggs. In another shallow bowl, combine the breadcrumbs and sesame seeds.

4. Cut the chilled grits into 2-inch squares. Dip each square first in the beaten egg and then in the breadcrumb and sesame seed mixture.

5. In a large skillet, melt the butter over medium-high heat. Add the grits squares and cook until golden brown, about 2½ minutes per side.   *8 servings*

Green Rice

The "green" ingredients may vary, depending upon your whim, but they should be compatible with the flavors in the main course you are planning to serve.

2 tablespoons butter
1 cup chopped leeks (about 1 medium), or
    1 cup chopped scallions (about 5 medium)
1 cup raw rice

1 cup water
1 cup canned chicken broth
⅓ cup chopped parsley
⅓ cup chopped fresh dill

1. In a medium saucepan, melt the butter over medium heat. Add the leeks and sauté until softened but not browned, about 7 minutes. Add the rice and cook, stirring, for 3 minutes longer.

2. Add the water and chicken broth. Increase the heat to medium-high and bring to a boil. Reduce the heat to medium-low, cover, and simmer until the rice is tender and all of the liquid is absorbed, about 20 minutes.

3. Stir in the parsley and dill, fluffing the rice with a fork.   *4 servings*

Sesame-Coated Fried Grits

Potato-Cheese Pancakes with Scallions

Potato pancakes are not made with a flour batter, as are other vegetable pancakes, because potatoes contain a sufficient amount of natural starch to hold the cakes together. Be sure to use all-purpose potatoes; waxy potatoes are not as starchy and have a higher moisture content, which results in a pancake that does not brown as well.

2 medium all-purpose potatoes (about ¾ pound)
2 eggs
1 cup grated Swiss cheese (about ¼ pound)
¼ cup chopped scallions (1 or 2 medium)
1 tablespoon chopped parsley

1 tablespoon flour
¼ teaspoon salt
¼ teaspoon pepper
2 tablespoons butter
2 tablespoons vegetable oil

1. Peel the potatoes and grate them. Pat the potatoes dry with paper towels.
2. In a medium bowl, beat the eggs. Stir in the potatoes, cheese, scallions, parsley, flour, salt, and pepper.
3. In a large skillet, heat 1 tablespoon of the butter in 1 tablespoon of the oil over medium-high heat. Drop the potato mixture by ½ cup into the skillet and flatten each cake with a spoon. Cook the cakes until browned, 5 to 6 minutes per side. Add the remaining butter and oil, if necessary, to prevent sticking.

4 servings

Savannah Red Rice

This dish is a specialty of Georgia and South Carolina (where it is simply called red rice). Cooks in other parts of the country will recognize it as Spanish rice.

6 slices bacon (about ¼ pound)
1 cup chopped scallions (about 5 medium)
1 small green bell pepper, chopped (about ¾ cup)
2 cups raw rice
1 can (14 ounces) whole tomatoes, with their juice
4 tablespoons tomato paste

½ teaspoon paprika
½ teaspoon sugar
½ teaspoon hot pepper sauce
¾ teaspoon salt
¼ teaspoon black pepper
1¾ cups canned chicken broth
⅓ cup water
2 tablespoons chopped parsley, for garnish

1. Preheat the oven to 325°.
2. In a large ovenproof skillet with a tight-fitting lid, cook the bacon, uncovered, over medium heat until crisp, about 10 minutes. Reserving the fat in the skillet, drain the bacon on paper towels; crumble and set aside.
3. In the bacon fat, sauté the scallions and green pepper over medium heat until the scallions are softened but not browned, about 5 minutes. Add the rice and cook, stirring, for 5 minutes.

4. Stir in the tomatoes with their juice, breaking them up with a spoon. Stir in the tomato paste, paprika, sugar, hot pepper sauce, salt, black pepper, chicken broth, and water. Increase the heat to medium-high and bring to a boil, stirring.

5. Cover and bake in the oven until the rice is tender and all of the liquid is absorbed, about 45 minutes.

6. Stir once and let stand, covered, for 10 minutes. Serve sprinkled with the reserved bacon and the parsley.   *6 servings*

Boston Baked Beans

This signature dish of Boston, Massachusetts, dates from the 17th century, when the Puritan sabbath—a day on which work was forbidden—was observed from sundown on Saturday until Sunday evening. The baked beans would be started on Saturday morning and then left to cook slowly until dinnertime so that the Puritan housewife did not have to break the sabbath to cook a meal. Leftover beans would then be served for Sunday breakfast or lunch. Boston baked beans were often baked in communal ovens by the local baker, who would collect bean pots from the townspeople on Saturday morning and return the pots of baked beans in time for dinner that night.

1 pound dried Great Northern beans, rinsed and picked over
2 medium onions, 1 peeled and left whole and 1 chopped
¼ pound salt pork, diced
⅔ cup molasses

3 tablespoons brown sugar
1 tablespoon dry mustard
1 teaspoon salt
½ teaspoon pepper
¼ teaspoon ground cloves
1 bay leaf

1. Soak the beans overnight in water to cover by 3 inches. Or, alternatively: place the beans in a saucepan with water to cover by 2 inches; bring to a boil and boil for 2 minutes; remove from the heat, cover, and let stand for 1 hour.

2. Drain the beans and place them in a large saucepan with 8 cups of water. Bring the beans to a boil over medium-high heat. Add the whole onion, reduce the heat to low, and simmer, partially covered, until the beans are half tender, about 30 minutes. Drain the beans and discard the onion.

3. Meanwhile, in a small saucepan of boiling water, blanch the salt pork for 3 minutes. Drain and set aside.

4. Preheat the oven to 250°.

5. In a bowl, combine the chopped onion with the molasses, brown sugar, dry mustard, salt, pepper, and cloves. Stir in 2 cups of water.

6. Place the beans and reserved salt pork in a 2½-quart casserole or bean pot. Add the bay leaf. Pour the onion-molasses mixture over the beans. Cover tightly and bake for 3½ hours.

7. Remove the cover, stir the beans, and continue baking, uncovered, for 30 minutes longer. Discard the bay leaf before serving.   *4 servings*

DRIED BEANS AND PEAS

Dried beans and peas, also known as legumes, have been an important staple in American cooking since colonial times. Long considered hearty peasant fare, today beans and peas are prized for their cholesterol-free protein and their high fiber content, and for the many appetizing ways in which they can be prepared.

Whether you choose classic Boston baked beans, Southwestern refried beans, or a simple Southern side dish of black-eyed peas, you must plan ahead: in general, legumes require long, slow cooking. Before cooking, pick over the beans or peas, discarding any foreign matter or discolored specimens, then rinse them well. Except for lentils and split peas, most legumes need an overnight soaking to rehydrate them. Never add salt to the soaking water; it toughens the legumes and prevents them from absorbing water. (It is said that changing the soaking water several times helps cut down on the flatulence caused by some beans.) After soaking, remove any specimens that float, drain the legumes, and add fresh water to cover. Slowly bring the beans or peas to a boil and simmer from one to several hours (lentils require only about 20 minutes).

Today supermarkets and health food stores stock a wide variety of beans and peas, such as those at right. At home, store dried legumes in airtight containers. A row of glass jars filled with them will add a colorful, decorative touch to any country kitchen.

Hoppin' John

Hoppin' John

Southerners serve Hoppin' John on New Year's Day to assure good luck for the following year. The origin of its name is unclear, although it may stem from a children's game that involved hopping around the table before eating the dish.

¼ pound bacon (4 to 6 slices)
1 medium onion, chopped (about 1¼ cups)
1 clove garlic, minced
1 cup raw rice
2 packages (10 ounces each) frozen
  black-eyed peas

2 cups water
1 teaspoon salt
1 medium tomato, chopped
  (about 1 cup)
2 tablespoons chopped parsley

1. In a medium saucepan, cook the bacon over medium heat until crisp, about 10 minutes. Reserving the fat in the saucepan, drain the bacon on paper towels; crumble and set aside.

2. In the bacon fat, sauté the onion and garlic over medium heat until the onion is softened but not browned, about 10 minutes.

3. Add the rice, black-eyed peas, water, and salt. Increase the heat to medium-high and bring to a boil. Reduce the heat to medium-low, cover, and cook until the rice is tender and the liquid is absorbed, 15 to 20 minutes.

4. Stir in the tomato, parsley, and the reserved bacon. Cover and cook over medium heat until heated through, about 2 minutes.   *6 servings*

Cajun Dirty Rice

Do not let the name deter you from trying this savory Louisiana classic. Although Dirty Rice is generally served as a side dish, it is fairly substantial and would make a satisfying main course for lunch or a light supper.

½ pound chicken gizzards
1¼ cups canned chicken broth
1 cup water
2 slices bacon
1 large green bell pepper, chopped
1 medium red bell pepper, chopped
1 medium onion, chopped (about 1¼ cups)
1 cup chopped scallions (about 5 medium)
2 medium carrots, chopped (about 1 cup)

¼ cup chopped parsley
2 cloves garlic, minced
½ teaspoon salt
¼ teaspoon black pepper
¼ teaspoon cayenne pepper
1 cup raw rice
2 tablespoons butter
½ pound chicken livers

1. In a medium saucepan, bring the gizzards, chicken broth, and water to a boil. Reduce the heat to medium-low, cover, and simmer until the gizzards are tender, about 45 minutes. Reserving the broth, remove the gizzards, and when they are cool enough to handle, mince them and set them aside.

2. In a Dutch oven or flameproof casserole, cook the bacon over medium heat until crisp, about 10 minutes. Reserving the fat in the pan, drain the bacon on paper towels; crumble and set aside.

3. In the bacon fat, sauté the gizzards over medium heat until browned, about 5 minutes.

4. Add the green and red bell peppers, the onion, scallions, carrots, parsley, garlic, salt, black pepper, and cayenne. Cook over medium heat until the vegetables have softened, about 5 minutes.

5. Add the rice and reserved broth. Increase the heat to medium-high and bring to a boil. Stir once, reduce the heat to medium-low, cover, and simmer until the rice is tender, about 15 minutes.

6. Meanwhile, in a medium skillet, melt the butter over medium heat. Add the chicken livers and sauté until firm, about 3 minutes. Let the livers cool slightly, then coarsely chop them. Toss the chicken livers and bacon with the rice. Cover and let sit for 10 minutes before serving.   *6 to 8 servings*

The word Cajun refers to the French Canadians, or Acadians, who emigrated to Louisiana in the 17th century. Creoles are Louisianians who are descended from French and Spanish colonists. Although the cuisines of both groups reflect similar influences, Creole is a more urban, refined cooking style while Cajun is a homey, country style of cooking.

Sheepherder's Potatoes

Basque shepherds, from the Pyrenees Mountains between France and Spain, came to this country in the early 20th century and settled in the mountains of Nevada, northern California, and Idaho, where there are still sizable Basque communities. With them they brought a cuisine that was not only a blend of Basque, French, and Spanish cultures, but also a reflection of their nomadic existence. This rustic potato dish is a perfect example: all of the ingredients are cooked together in a skillet, as you would do if you were cooking dinner over a campfire. If this "shepherd's pie" were being cooked in one of the many boardinghouses that served the shepherds, leftover meat would also have been added to the pan for a heartier dish.

*6 medium all-purpose potatoes (about
   2 pounds)*
¼ pound bacon (4 to 6 slices)
1 cup chopped leeks or onions
4 eggs

2 tablespoons milk
2 tablespoons chopped parsley
½ teaspoon thyme
½ teaspoon salt
¼ teaspoon pepper

    1. In a large saucepan of simmering salted water, cook the potatoes until almost tender, 35 to 40 minutes. When the potatoes are cool enough to handle, peel them and cut them crosswise into ⅛-inch slices. Set aside.

    2. Preheat the oven to 375°.

    3. In a large ovenproof skillet, preferably nonstick (see Note), cook the bacon over medium heat until crisp, about 10 minutes. Reserving the fat in the skillet, drain the bacon on paper towels; crumble and set aside.

    4. In the bacon fat, sauté the leeks over medium heat until softened but not browned, about 7 minutes.

    5. Carefully add the potato slices and gently toss them with the leeks. Shake the potatoes until they lie in a thick, flat layer in the pan. Cook the potatoes over medium heat until the bottom of the layer is golden brown, about 10 minutes.

    6. Meanwhile, in a medium bowl, beat the eggs with the milk, parsley, thyme, salt, and pepper. Pour the eggs over the potatoes and sprinkle the reserved bacon on top. Place in the oven and bake until the eggs are set, 5 to 7 minutes.

    7. Serve directly from the skillet. *4 servings*

NOTE: If you are not using a nonstick pan, it may be necessary to add a little oil or butter to keep the potatoes from sticking in Step 5.

Sheepherder's Potatoes

Red Beans and Rice

In New Orleans, this dish is often made with a ham bone. If you happen to have one, cook it with the beans in Step 2. When it is cool enough to handle, remove the meat from the bone and use it in place of the diced ham.

*1 pound dried red beans or red kidney beans,
   rinsed and picked over*
3½ cups canned beef broth
2 medium onions, chopped (about 2½ cups)
2 stalks celery, chopped (about 1 cup)
¼ pound ham, diced (about 1 cup)
4 cloves garlic, minced

1 teaspoon thyme
1 bay leaf
½ teaspoon hot pepper sauce
*½ pound hot Italian sausage,
   casings removed*
Steamed rice
¼ cup chopped parsley, for garnish

   1. Soak the beans overnight in water to cover by 3 inches. Or, alternatively: Place the beans in a saucepan with water to cover by 2 inches; bring to a boil and boil for 2 minutes. Remove from the heat, cover, and let stand for 1 hour.

   2. Drain the beans. Place them in a large saucepan or soup pot and add the beef broth and 2 cups of water. Bring to a boil over medium-high heat. Reduce the heat to medium-low, cover, and simmer until the beans are tender, about 1 hour. Add more water, if necessary, to keep the beans covered.

   3. Increase the heat to medium-high. Add the onions, celery, ham, garlic, thyme, bay leaf, hot pepper sauce, and enough water to cover the beans. Break the sausage into bite-size pieces and add to the pot. Bring the mixture to a boil; reduce the heat to medium-low and simmer, partially covered, until the liquid has thickened, about 1½ hours.

   4. Remove the bay leaf. Serve the beans over rice and sprinkled with the parsley.

8 servings

Hashed Brown Potatoes

Even if the hashed brown potato was not actually invented in this country (there is some argument that it is based on a Swiss dish called *rösti*), short-order cooks have made this ubiquitous diner dish a purely American institution.

2 pounds boiling potatoes
1 small onion, chopped (about 1 cup)
1 cup chopped scallions (about 5 medium)
1 teaspoon salt

½ teaspoon pepper
¼ pound bacon (4 to 6 slices)
3 tablespoons butter

   1. In a large saucepan of simmering salted water, cook the potatoes until tender, 30 to 35 minutes. Drain well, return to the saucepan, and shake over medium heat until they are dry. Remove from the heat and when they are cool enough to handle, peel them, and cut into ½-inch dice.

2. In a large bowl, toss the potatoes, onion, scallions, salt, and pepper together.

3. In a large skillet, preferably nonstick (see Note), cook the bacon over medium heat until crisp, about 10 minutes. Reserving the fat in the skillet, drain the bacon on paper towels; crumble and set aside.

4. Add the butter to the bacon fat and heat over medium-high heat. Add the potato mixture and press firmly into the pan with a spatula. Cook, flipping frequently, until the potatoes brown, 10 to 15 minutes.

5. Serve hot with the crumbled bacon on top.   *4 servings*

NOTE: If you are not using a nonstick skillet, it may be necessary to add more butter to keep the potatoes from sticking in Step 4.

Stuffed Baked Potatoes

The onion, green pepper, and tomato add wonderful flavor and texture to the creamy and rich stuffing for these baked potatoes.

4 large baking potatoes (about 2½ pounds)
2 tablespoons butter
¼ pound bacon (4 to 6 slices)
½ cup finely chopped onion
½ cup finely chopped green bell pepper
½ cup chopped tomato, well drained

¼ cup sour cream
1 egg yolk
¼ teaspoon black pepper
1 cup grated Swiss or Cheddar cheese
* (about ¼ pound)*

1. Preheat the oven to 425°.

2. Prick the potatoes with the tines of a fork and rub the skins with the butter. Bake until the potatoes are tender, about 1 hour.

3. Meanwhile, in a medium skillet, cook the bacon over medium heat until crisp, about 10 minutes. Reserving the fat in the skillet, drain the bacon on paper towels; crumble and set aside.

4. In the bacon fat, sauté the onion over medium heat for 5 minutes. Add the green pepper and tomato and cook until the onion is softened but not browned, about 5 minutes longer. Set aside.

5. When the potatoes are done, remove them from the oven and lower the oven temperature to 375°. Cut a ¼-inch-thick horizontal slice from a long side of each potato. Scoop out the inside of the potato, leaving a ¼-inch shell.

6. Place the potato pulp in a bowl and mash it to a smooth purée with a fork. Beat in the sour cream, egg yolk, and black pepper. Stir in the reserved vegetable mixture and bacon.

7. Spoon the mashed potato mixture into the potato shells. Place the potatoes in a baking dish, sprinkle the cheese on top, and bake until the tops are golden brown, about 10 minutes.   *4 servings*

Grits and Swiss Cheese Casserole

Hominy grits baked with cheese is a Southern side dish often served with game birds, although it goes well with any roast meat or poultry.

2 cups milk
2 cups water
⅓ cup butter
2 cloves garlic, minced
½ teaspoon salt
¼ teaspoon pepper

1 cup grits
2 cups grated Swiss cheese (about
 ½ pound)
1 cup chopped scallions (about 5 medium)
3 eggs, lightly beaten

Make a lighter version of traditional scalloped potatoes by replacing the cream or milk with chicken stock. Layer the sliced potatoes in a shallow baking dish with one and a half cups of chicken stock, two tablespoons of butter, dried herbs, and salt and pepper to taste. Bake in a 400° oven, uncovered, for about an hour, until the potatoes are tender.

1. Preheat the oven to 350°. Butter a 1½-quart baking dish.
2. In a large saucepan, bring the milk, water, butter, garlic, salt, and pepper to a boil. Gradually stir in the grits. Reduce the heat to medium-low and simmer, uncovered, stirring frequently until thick, about 5 minutes. Stir in the cheese and scallions and remove from the heat.
3. Place the eggs in a bowl. Stir about 1 cup of the hot grits into the eggs and stir the warmed eggs into the remaining grits in the saucepan.
4. Pour the grits into the prepared baking dish and spread evenly. Bake until the grits are set and golden brown on top, 35 to 40 minutes. Let stand for 10 minutes before serving.

6 servings

Scalloped New Potatoes

Scalloped potatoes are best made with waxy, or boiling, potatoes, which retain their firm texture during cooking. For a simple variation on this recipe, sprinkle some thyme, basil, or tarragon over the potatoes before baking.

2 tablespoons flour
1 teaspoon salt
½ teaspoon pepper, preferably white
2½ pounds small red potatoes, peeled
 and cut into ⅛-inch slices

1 cup chopped scallions (about 5 medium)
1 teaspoon minced garlic
3 tablespoons butter
2 cups light cream or half-and-half

1. Preheat the oven to 350°. Butter a 2- to 2½-quart baking dish.
2. In a small bowl, combine the flour, salt, and pepper.
3. Layer half of the potatoes in the bottom of the prepared baking dish. Sprinkle half the scallions and garlic on top. Sprinkle evenly with the seasoned flour. Repeat with the remaining potatoes, scallions, and garlic. Dot with the butter.
4. In a small saucepan, heat the cream until steaming but not boiling. Pour the hot cream over the potatoes and bake, uncovered, until the potatoes are tender and the top is browned, about 1 hour and 15 minutes.

4 to 6 servings

Wild Rice Medley

Wild Rice Medley

With their similar chewy textures and nutty tastes, wild rice and brown rice make ideal companions in this satisfying side dish. The recipe could also be used as a stuffing for poultry: it makes enough to stuff a 12-pound turkey, or a large roasting chicken with leftover stuffing to be baked separately.

1 cup raw brown rice
½ cup raw wild rice, rinsed
1½ cups canned chicken broth
1½ cups water
4 tablespoons butter
1 medium onion, chopped (about 1¼ cups)

1 clove garlic, minced
½ pound mushrooms, chopped (about 2 cups)
2 medium carrots, diced (about 1 cup)
½ cup chopped parsley

1. Place the brown rice, wild rice, chicken broth, and water in a large saucepan. Bring to a boil over medium-high heat. Reduce the heat to medium-low, cover, and simmer until the rice is tender and the liquid is absorbed, 35 to 40 minutes.

2. In a large skillet, melt the butter over medium heat. Add the onion and garlic and sauté until the onion is softened but not browned, about 10 minutes.

3. Add the mushrooms and carrots and continue cooking until the carrots are softened, about 5 minutes.

4. Add the cooked rice and the parsley to the skillet and toss to combine.

4 to 6 servings

WILD RICE

For most Americans, wild rice is a recently acquired taste. Until the mid-1960s, few people had eaten this nutty-flavored delicacy because it was not widely available. Today, more efficient methods of growing, harvesting, and processing wild rice mean that more people can enjoy this nutritious grain.

Wild rice, in fact, is not rice at all, but the grainlike seed of a grass that once grew only in the shallow waters of lakes in the north-central United States and parts of southern Canada. For the Indians (mainly Chippewas) who lived in these areas five hundred years ago, wild rice was the major source of carbohydrate in their diet.

Harvesting the rice, done mainly by women, was an autumn ritual for the Indians. Each day they poled their canoes carefully through the stands of ripening rice. A woman in the bow of each canoe thrust a pointed stick into the rice, bending the stalks over the gunwales; with an-

other stick she beat the stalks to release the grains.

Once gathered, the rice was generally cured by laying it on blankets in the sun for several days, or on racks over a fire. Or it was placed in a tub or kettle and stirred constantly over a slow fire until it was completely parched.

After curing, the rice was threshed to remove the tough hulls. This was usually done by youths, who trod on the grains in a large tub or in a skin-

lined hole in the ground. Sometimes the hard hulls were beaten off with heavy sticks. The hulls were then separated from the grain, or winnowed, usually by pouring the mixture from one basket to another during a stiff wind; the wind would blow the lighter chaff away.

Wild rice was cultivated in this manner until just a few decades ago. And while some Indians still pursue the "canoe and flail" method, today most wild rice—despite its name—is grown in paddies in Minnesota and California, and machine-processed.

Even with modern production methods, wild rice is still a notoriously difficult crop to grow, and its relatively high price reflects this problem. Nevertheless, supplies of wild rice have increased more than 1,000 percent since the 1960s, and it is not surprising to find this delicious food working its way off the shelves of gourmet food stores and onto weekday dining tables.

Various aspects of wild rice production by the Chippewa Indians of Minnesota are depicted in photos dating from the 1920s to the 1940s. Clockwise from bottom left: curing rice in a tub over a slow fire; tending a basket of hulled rice; winnowing the chaff in a basket; treading on the grains to hull them; bagging the grain; harvesting by the "canoe and flail" method; removing the tough hulls with sticks; poling home after a day of harvesting.

Breads and Biscuits

great for spreading with butter

or sopping up gravy

Be it brown bread, cornbread, monkey bread, or cream biscuits, there is nothing more tantalizing than the smell of fresh bread baking in the oven. But baking bread has not always been the pleasure it is today. Before the 19th century brought the invention of reliable leavening agents, cooks were forced to use a variety of ingredients to lighten their breads. Yeast was made from such things as hops, grated potatoes, and tree leaves, and quick breads were leavened by tediously beating air into the eggs or by adding water in which hardwood ashes had been soaked. Even if the mix was right, breads often failed because fires and woodstoves were difficult to regulate.

As the recipes in this chapter show, baking bread is a far less arduous task than in the past. Cooks today have baking powder and packaged yeast to lighten their creations—and trustworthy ovens produce dependable results. So easy and comforting is breadmaking, in fact, that many cooks do it to relax.

A food safe protects freshly baked country breads and biscuits.

Sweet Potato Monkey Bread

Monkey bread, also called bubble bread, has a distinctive shape. It is formed by dividing a yeast dough into small pieces, rolling the pieces into balls, coating the balls in butter or a butter-sugar glaze (so that they will remain separate as they bake), and layering them in a mold. Other ingredients, such as currants or nuts, can be added to the dough or to the glaze.

1 large sweet potato
1 cup milk
1 package active dry yeast
¾ cup (packed) dark brown sugar
1 tablespoon unsulphured molasses

6 tablespoons butter, melted
¾ teaspoon salt
1½ cups currants
About 2½ cups flour
1 cup chopped walnuts

1. In a large saucepan of simmering salted water, cook the sweet potato until tender, 30 to 35 minutes. When it is cool enough to handle, peel the sweet potato, and mash it well with a fork. Measure out ⅓ cup of mashed sweet potato (if there is any remaining, reserve it for another use).

2. In a small saucepan, scald the milk. Pour the milk into a large bowl and when it has cooled to lukewarm (105° to 115°), sprinkle the yeast on top, then let it sit 1 or 2 minutes before stirring to dissolve.

3. To the milk, add ¼ cup of the brown sugar, the molasses, 2 tablespoons of the butter, and the salt. Stir in the currants and the mashed sweet potato. Stir in enough flour, 1 cup at a time, to make a soft dough. Turn the dough out onto a floured surface and knead lightly until smooth and elastic, about 10 minutes, adding more flour, if necessary, to keep the dough from sticking. Form the dough into a ball and transfer it to a greased bowl; turn the dough to coat the surface. Cover the bowl with plastic wrap, set it aside in a warm draft-free place, and let the dough rise until it doubles in bulk, about 1 hour and 30 minutes. Generously butter a 10-inch tube or bundt pan (do not use a pan with a removable bottom).

4. Just before the dough has doubled in bulk, prepare the glaze. In a small saucepan, melt the remaining 4 tablespoons butter and the remaining ½ cup brown sugar over medium heat, stirring to dissolve the sugar. Keep warm over low heat.

5. When the dough has doubled, punch it down, turn it out onto a lightly floured surface, and knead lightly until no longer sticky, adding more flour if necessary. Divide the dough into 18 equal pieces and roll the pieces into balls.

6. Pour half of the warm (but not hot) glaze into the bottom of the prepared tube pan and then sprinkle on half the nuts. Place half of the dough balls over the nuts in the pan. Drizzle the remaining warm glaze over the dough balls and sprinkle with the remaining nuts. Top with the remaining balls of dough. Cover the pan loosely with plastic wrap and set it aside in a warm draft-free place until the dough has almost doubled, about 30 minutes.

7. Preheat the oven to 350°.

8. Bake the monkey bread until nicely browned, about 35 minutes. Let it cool in the pan for 5 to 10 minutes and then serve warm. *Makes one 10-inch round loaf*

Sweet Potato Monkey Bread

Chili·Cheddar Cornbread

In colonial days, cornbread would have been cooked over an open fire in a cast-iron skillet or in a special three-legged frying pan called a spider. Today, cornbread can still be made in a skillet, but it is usually baked in the oven instead of on top of the stove. Here, the cornbread is accented with fresh hot peppers and cheese.

1 cup yellow cornmeal
¾ cup flour
2 tablespoons sugar
1½ teaspoons baking powder
½ teaspoon baking soda
½ teaspoon salt
1 cup buttermilk

2 eggs, lightly beaten
1 cup corn kernels, fresh (about 2 ears), or
    frozen, thawed
1 cup grated Cheddar cheese (about ¼ pound)
1 small fresh jalapeño pepper, seeded and
    minced (see Note, page 43)
3 tablespoons butter

1. Preheat the oven to 425°.
2. In a large bowl, combine the cornmeal, flour, sugar, baking powder, baking soda, and salt. In another bowl, blend the buttermilk with the eggs. Stir the wet ingredients into the dry ingredients. Stir in the corn, cheese, and jalapeño.
3. In an 8-inch ovenproof skillet or 8-inch square baking pan, melt the butter. Swirl the butter in the pan to coat the bottom and sides, then pour the remaining butter into the batter and stir to combine. Pour the batter into the skillet, spread evenly, and bake for 20 to 25 minutes, or until the cornbread is golden and a toothpick inserted in the center comes out clean.   *8 servings*

Anadama Bread

A specialty of New England, anadama bread was inadvertently named—or so numerous sources claim—by a Gloucester, Massachusetts, fisherman. One day he grew so frustrated with the meal of cornmeal and molasses that his wife, Anna, served him every night that he added some yeast and flour to the mixture, stuck it in the oven to bake, and muttered, as he ate the resulting bread, "Anna, damn her!"

1½ cups boiling water
½ cup yellow cornmeal
⅓ cup dark unsulphured molasses
3 tablespoons butter, plus 2 tablespoons
    melted butter

¾ teaspoon salt
1 package active dry yeast
1 egg, lightly beaten
5¾ to 6 cups flour

1. In a large bowl, combine the boiling water, cornmeal, molasses, the 3 tablespoons of butter, and the salt. Let cool to lukewarm (105° to 115°), about 15 minutes.
2. Sprinkle the yeast over the lukewarm mixture and let it sit for 1 or 2 minutes

before stirring to dissolve. Then stir in the egg and 3 cups of the flour. Stir in another 2¾ cups flour until the dough forms a soft ball.

3. Turn the dough out onto a lightly floured surface and knead until smooth, about 10 minutes, adding up to ¼ cup more flour, if necessary, to keep the dough from sticking. Form the dough into a ball and transfer it to a greased bowl; turn the dough to coat the surface. Cover the bowl with plastic wrap, set it aside in a warm draft-free place, and let the dough rise until it doubles in bulk, 50 to 60 minutes.

4. Butter two 9 x 5-inch loaf pans. Punch the dough down, turn out onto a lightly floured surface, and knead lightly for 1 minute. Shape the dough into two loaves and place in the prepared pans. Set the loaves aside in a warm draft-free place and let the dough rise, uncovered, until it doubles in bulk, about 45 minutes.

5. Preheat the oven to 350°.

6. Brush the loaves with the 2 tablespoons melted butter. Bake until the tops are golden brown and the bread sounds hollow when thumped on the bottom, about 30 minutes. Cool the loaves in the pans for 10 minutes and then turn them out onto a rack to cool completely before slicing.   *Makes 2 loaves*

Sally Lunn

A staple of the Southern tea table, this egg-rich and slightly sweet yeast bread is also delicious when sliced and used for sandwiches or toast. Sally Lunn is apparently named for an Englishwoman who sold the bread (as rolls) in the city of Bath.

¼ cup lukewarm (105° to 115°) water	*½ teaspoon salt*
1 package active dry yeast	*1 cup milk*
1 stick (4 ounces) plus 2 tablespoons butter	*3 eggs, lightly beaten*
3 tablespoons sugar	*4½ cups flour*

1. Place the water in a small bowl and sprinkle the yeast on top to dissolve.

2. Place the butter, sugar, and salt in a medium bowl. In a small saucepan, heat the milk to almost boiling and pour over the butter, sugar, and salt. Let the milk mixture cool to lukewarm (105° to 115°).

3. Stir the eggs, dissolved yeast, and 3 cups of the flour into the lukewarm milk mixture. Stir in enough additional flour, about 1½ cups, to make a soft but sticky dough.

4. Place the dough in a heavily buttered 10-inch bundt pan. Cover the pan with plastic wrap, set aside in a warm draft-free place, and let the dough rise until it doubles in bulk, about 1 hour.

5. Preheat the oven to 400°.

6. Bake the bread for 15 minutes. Lower the oven temperature to 350° and bake for 15 to 20 minutes longer, or until the top is light golden and the bread sounds hollow when thumped on the bottom. Cool the bread in the pan for 10 minutes, then turn it out onto a rack to cool completely before slicing.   *Makes one 10-inch round loaf*

SHAPED BREADS

COTTAGE LOAF

Like many country breads, the traditional cottage loaf is baked freeform. Its shape comes from one ball of dough being stacked on top of another, which creates more surface area and therefore plenty of tasty crust. Start with any standard recipe for yeast bread dough that makes about a 9 x 5-inch loaf. After the initial kneading, let the dough rise until doubled in bulk, punch it down, and proceed with the technique shown at right.

Using a dough scraper or a large, sharp chef's knife, cut the dough into two pieces, making one piece approximately twice the size of the other piece.

Shape each piece into a smooth ball by holding it in one hand and pinching the dough into the middle with the other. Turn the ball over and pat it into a smooth round.

BRAIDED LOAF

Braiding is a simple way to add visual appeal to a bread. The number of strands can range from three to nine. Start with any standard recipe for yeast bread dough (or for an egg-enriched yeast dough, such as that for challah) that makes about a 9 x 5-inch loaf. After the initial kneading, let the dough rise until doubled in bulk; then punch it down, divide it into three equal pieces, and proceed with the technique shown at right.

Roughly shape the dough into three cylinders; let them rest for about 15 minutes. With the palms of your hands, roll the cylinders into strands of equal length.

Lay the three strands of dough side by side on a greased baking sheet. Start braiding the strands in the middle of the loaf and work toward one end.

NOTCHED LOAF

One way to give bread a rustic, country look is to coat it with flour before baking. For this loaf, the flour accentuates a design cut into the dough, a technique often used in making sourdough bread. Start with any standard recipe for yeast bread dough that makes about a 9 x 5-inch loaf. After the initial kneading, let the dough rise until doubled in bulk, punch it down, and proceed with the technique shown at right.

Shape the dough into a smooth ball (see the second step of Cottage Loaf, above). Place the dough on a greased baking sheet and coat the loaf liberally with flour.

Let the dough rise until doubled in bulk. Then, using sharp scissors, create scallops by making eight evenly spaced 2-inch-deep cuts into the circumference of the dough.

Let the balls of dough rest for 10 minutes, then make a hole through the center of each by pressing two fingers straight through to the work surface.

Let the dough rest for another 15 minutes, then stack the two rings, centering the holes. Press two fingers through the holes, straight through to the work surface.

Place the dough on a greased baking sheet and let it rise until it has doubled in bulk. Bake the cottage loaf in a 450° oven for 30 to 40 minutes, or until browned.

Firmly pinch the ends of the strands together to seal the braid. Then continue braiding toward the other end of the loaf and repeat the pinching process.

Let the loaf rise until doubled in bulk. To give it a rich color and sheen, brush the risen loaf with a glaze of egg yolk beaten with about 2 teaspoons of water.

Bake the loaf in a 450° oven for 30 to 40 minutes, or until browned. For a crisper crust, place a pan of boiling water on the bottom of the oven for the first 15 minutes.

To exaggerate the scalloped effect of the loaf when baked, tuck the corners of each scallop under the loaf to increase the space between the scallops.

Using a small, sharp paring knife, score a circle in the center of the loaf. Then score the circle into eighths so that the scores correspond to the original scallop-edge cuts.

Bake the loaf in a 400° oven for 15 minutes; lower the temperature to 350° and bake for another 20 minutes; then bake for a final 15 minutes, or until browned, at 325°.

Sopaipillas

Sopaipillas

In New Mexico, sopaipillas are often dredged in cinnamon sugar (as here) and eaten for breakfast or dessert. This puffed fried bread can also be served plain as a side dish or stuffed with a savory filling for a main course.

¼ cup sugar	½ teaspoon salt
2 teaspoons cinnamon	2 tablespoons chilled butter
2 cups flour	⅔ cup water
2 teaspoons baking powder	6 to 8 cups peanut oil, for deep-frying

    1. In a small bowl, combine the sugar and cinnamon, and set aside.

    2. In a large bowl, combine the flour, baking powder, and salt. Cut in the butter until the mixture resembles coarse meal. Sprinkle on the water, tossing with a fork until the dough is just moistened and crumbly.

    3. Turn the dough out onto a floured surface and knead until smooth. Form the dough into a ball and let stand for 10 minutes.

    4. In a Dutch oven or deep-fryer, heat 2 inches of oil to 375° over medium heat.

    5. Roll the dough into a rectangle ¼ inch thick and cut the dough into 2½-inch squares.

    6. Add the dough squares, a few at a time, to the hot oil and fry, gently turning with tongs to brown evenly, until they are puffed and golden, 2 to 4 minutes. Drain the squares on paper towels and while they are still hot, dredge them in the sugar-cinnamon mixture. *Makes about 3 dozen*

Ham and Scallion Biscuits

If you would prefer to make simple buttermilk biscuits, without the ham and scallions, increase the salt to ½ teaspoon and decrease the buttermilk to ½ cup.

2 cups flour
2 teaspoons baking powder
½ teaspoon baking soda
½ teaspoon sugar
¼ teaspoon salt

¼ teaspoon pepper
⅓ cup chilled butter, cut into pieces
1 cup minced ham (about ¼ pound)
½ cup minced scallions (2 to 3 medium)
¾ cup buttermilk

1. Preheat the oven to 400°.
2. In a large bowl, blend the flour, baking powder, baking soda, sugar, salt, and pepper. Cut in the butter until the mixture resembles coarse crumbs. Stir in the ham and scallions.
3. Sprinkle on the buttermilk, tossing the mixture with a fork until it forms a soft dough. Turn the dough out onto a lightly floured surface and roll the dough out ½ inch thick. Cut out biscuits with a floured 2-inch round biscuit or cookie cutter.
4. Bake the biscuits on ungreased baking sheets for 20 to 25 minutes, or until the tops are golden brown.   *Makes about 20*

Nut Popovers

Unlike many whimsically titled dishes, the origin of the popover's name is hardly mysterious. When the Yorkshire-puddinglike egg batter is baked in the cups of a popover tin, it rises up and "pops" over the top.

1 cup milk
2 eggs, lightly beaten
2 tablespoons butter, melted
¾ cup all-purpose flour
¼ cup whole wheat flour

½ teaspoon salt
2 tablespoons finely chopped toasted pine nuts
  (see Note)
2 tablespoons finely chopped toasted almonds
  (see Note)

1. Preheat the oven to 425°. Heavily butter a 6-cup nonstick popover pan.
2. In a mixing bowl, blend the milk, eggs, butter, all-purpose and whole wheat flours, and the salt. Stir in the toasted nuts.
3. Fill each popover cup two-thirds full with the batter and bake for 25 to 30 minutes, or until the popovers are puffed and golden on top. Serve hot.   *Makes 6*

NOTE: Place the pine nuts and almonds on an ungreased cookie sheet and bake in a 375° oven for 10 minutes, or until golden. Allow the nuts to cool before chopping them.

Popovers are delicious for breakfast, served hot with butter and jam; they also make an elegant alternative to a standard sandwich. Fill popovers with chicken or seafood salad and garnish each plate with sliced fruit; or stuff them with thinly sliced country ham, grated Cheddar, and a little mustard for a festive brunch entrée.

Cranberry-Almond Bread

Cranberries have been a part of this country's culinary heritage since the early 17th century, when Indians cooked this native American fruit in maple sugar or honey to make a condiment for meat and poultry. As in colonial days, cranberries are still available fresh only in the fall, but they can be successfully frozen for later use and added to recipes such as this without defrosting.

2 cups flour
¾ cup sugar
2 teaspoons baking powder
½ teaspoon salt
¾ cup milk
6 tablespoons butter, melted

1 egg, lightly beaten
1 tablespoon grated orange zest
1 teaspoon almond extract
1 cup fresh or frozen cranberries
1 cup sliced almonds

1. Preheat the oven to 325°. Butter a 9 x 5-inch loaf pan.
2. In a large bowl, blend the flour, sugar, baking powder, and salt. In another bowl, combine the milk, melted butter, egg, orange zest, and almond extract. Add the wet ingredients to the dry ingredients and stir just until no streaks of flour remain. Fold in the cranberries and almonds.
3. Pour the batter into the prepared loaf pan and spread evenly. Bang the pan once or twice on the counter to remove any air pockets. Bake for 1 hour and 10 minutes, or until the top is golden and a toothpick inserted in the center of the bread comes out clean. Cool the bread in the pan for 10 minutes and then turn it out onto a rack to cool completely before slicing.

Makes 1 loaf

To make an emergency substitute for baking powder, add 2 teaspoons cream of tartar, 1 teaspoon baking soda, and ¼ teaspoon salt for each cup of flour in the recipe. Although homemade powder is just as effective as commercial baking powder, it does not keep well, so do not plan to make a batch and store it.

Southern Cream Biscuits with Parsley

It is the heavy cream in these popular baking powder biscuits that makes them flaky and rich tasting. For a simple variation, substitute chives for the parsley.

2 cups flour
2 teaspoons baking powder
½ teaspoon salt

4 tablespoons chilled butter, cut into pieces
⅓ cup chopped parsley
1 cup heavy cream

1. Preheat the oven to 450°.
2. In a large bowl, blend the flour, baking powder, and salt. Cut in the butter until the mixture resembles coarse crumbs. Stir in the parsley.
3. Sprinkle on the cream, tossing the mixture with a fork until it forms a soft dough. Turn the dough out onto a lightly floured surface and roll it out ½ inch thick. Cut out biscuits with a floured 2½-inch round biscuit or cookie cutter.
4. Bake the biscuits on ungreased baking sheets for 10 to 12 minutes, or until the tops are golden brown.

Makes about 1 dozen

Cranberry-Almond Bread

Boston Brown Bread

This traditional companion to Boston Baked Beans (page 111) is also called "thirded" bread because it is made with one-third rye flour, one-third cornmeal, and one-third wheat flour. Although this bread has been around since the 17th century, the contemporary version gets its familiar cylindrical shape from the one-pound commercial coffee can—a modern convenience—in which it is usually steamed.

2 cups buttermilk
½ cup unsulphured molasses
½ cup golden raisins
½ cup dark raisins
1 cup rye flour

1 cup all-purpose flour
1 cup yellow cornmeal
1½ teaspoons baking soda
¾ teaspoon salt

1. In a large bowl, combine the buttermilk and molasses. Stir in the golden and dark raisins. In another bowl, blend the rye and all-purpose flours, cornmeal, baking soda, and salt. Stir the dry ingredients into the wet ingredients, 1 cup at a time, stirring well after each addition.

2. Heavily butter the insides of two 1-pound coffee cans. Pour the batter into the cans (the batter should come to within 2½ inches of the tops) and bang them lightly once or twice on the counter to settle the batter and remove any air pockets. Place a circle of buttered wax paper on top of the batter, cover each can loosely with foil, and tie the foil in place with string.

3. Stand the cans on a rack set in a large, deep pot with a cover. Pour in enough boiling water to come about three-fourths of the way up the sides of the cans. Return the water to a boil over high heat. Reduce the heat to low, cover the pot, and simmer for 2 hours and 15 minutes, adding more water if necessary to maintain the level.

4. To serve the bread immediately, remove the foil and wax paper, and unmold. Or leave the bread in the cans and then reheat before serving by steaming for 10 to 15 minutes.
Makes 2 loaves

Beaten Biscuits

To get the hard, dense texture of an authentic Southern beaten biscuit, cooks had to pound the dough with a mallet 200 times, or put it through a machine—specifically designed for the purpose—that resembled the wringers on an old-fashioned washing machine. Today, beaten biscuit dough can be made quickly in a food processor.

2 cups flour
½ teaspoon sugar
½ teaspoon salt
¼ teaspoon baking powder
4 tablespoons chilled butter, cut into pieces

4 tablespoons chilled lard or shortening,
    cut into pieces
¼ cup ice water
¼ cup milk

1. Preheat the oven to 350°.

2. In a food processor, combine the flour, sugar, salt, and baking powder, and process briefly to blend. Add the butter and lard, and process, turning the machine on and off, until the mixture resembles coarse meal.

3. Pour in the ice water and milk, and process briefly, just until the dough forms a ball. If the dough is too dry, add more water; if it is too wet, add more flour. Knead the dough in the food processor for 2 to 3 minutes.

4. On a lightly floured surface, roll the dough out ¼ inch thick. Fold the dough in half, pressing the two halves lightly together, and cut into 2-inch rounds with a floured biscuit cutter. Gather up the scraps, roll out to a ¼-inch thickness, fold in half, and cut out more biscuits. Repeat until all the scraps are used. Prick each biscuit with a fork.

5. Bake the biscuits on an ungreased baking sheet for 30 minutes, or until they are crisp but not browned. Serve the biscuits split in two. *Makes 10 to 12*

Pumpkin-Pine Nut Bread

This moist, orange-colored quick bread can also be made with butternut squash. To do so, halve and seed a medium-size squash and bake it, cut sides down, in a 375° oven until tender (about 30 minutes). Scoop out the flesh, mash it, and then cook it, stirring, over low heat until the squash is as thick as canned pumpkin purée.

*1 stick (4 ounces) butter, softened to room
    temperature*
¾ cup (packed) dark brown sugar
2 eggs
1 cup canned unsweetened solid-pack pumpkin
½ teaspoon orange extract

2 cups flour
2 teaspoons baking powder
½ teaspoon cinnamon
½ teaspoon ground ginger
⅓ cup milk
¾ cup pine nuts, toasted (see Note)

1. Preheat the oven to 350°. Butter a 9 x 5-inch loaf pan.

2. In a large mixing bowl, cream the butter and brown sugar. Beat in the eggs, pumpkin, and orange extract.

3. In a medium bowl, combine the flour, baking powder, cinnamon, and ginger. Add the dry ingredients and the milk, alternately, to the pumpkin mixture, and beat until just blended. Fold in the pine nuts.

4. Pour the batter into the prepared pan and spread evenly. Bang the pan once or twice on the counter to remove any air pockets. Bake for 1 hour to 1 hour and 10 minutes, or until the bread is golden and a toothpick inserted in the center comes out clean. Cool the bread in the pan for 10 minutes, then turn it out onto a rack to cool completely before slicing. *Makes 1 loaf*

NOTE: To toast the pine nuts, place them on an ungreased cookie sheet in a preheated 375° oven for 10 minutes, or until golden.

SEVEN

Desserts

*pies, cakes, ice creams,
puddings . . . and more*

Americans have always had a fondness for sweets. But whereas some cake recipes once called for forty eggs, and dessert tables brimmed with all manner of rich pastries and sweetmeats, contemporary dessert lovers are more circumspect in their demands.

Still, many of the desserts our forebears favored continue to be popular. This chapter includes recipes for such time-honored classics as Indian Pudding, Robert E. Lee Cake—a white cake that was supposedly the general's passion—and of course apple pie. With hundreds of varieties of apples available, including such long-forgotten types as Winter Banana and Sweet Bough, it was not uncommon for most early American housewives to have their own prized recipes for apple pie. Consequently, few early cookbooks bother to include this dessert.

Recipes for ice cream, however, were more commonly written down. It is said that Thomas Jefferson brought ice cream recipes back from his trips to France and Italy and served this dessert often at Monticello. This chapter offers two ice creams that may well have been Jefferson's favorites: rum-raisin and peaches and cream; both are a fitting end to almost any country meal.

The all-time favorite country dessert: apple pie.

Lemon Chess Pie

The filling for this classic Southern pie is similar to lemon curd; both are mixtures in which lemon juice is used to thicken, or curdle, beaten eggs. While lemon juice is the most common flavoring for chess pie, other chess pies use such sour ingredients as buttermilk or vinegar in its place.

Pie Pastry (below)
4 tablespoons butter, softened to
   room temperature
¾ cup sugar

2 tablespoons yellow cornmeal
5 eggs
1 tablespoon grated lemon zest
¼ cup lemon juice

The name chess pie may have come from the words "pie chest," another term for a pie safe, a type of food storage cabinet popular in the 19th and 20th centuries. The good keeping qualities of this pie probably led to its being called "chest pie" and eventually chess pie.

1. Make the Pie Pastry.
2. Preheat the oven to 325°.
3. In a medium bowl, cream the butter and sugar. Beat in the cornmeal.
4. Add the eggs, one at a time, beating well after each addition. Beat in the lemon zest and lemon juice.
5. Pour the mixture into the pie shell and bake for 45 minutes, or until a knife inserted in the center comes out clean. Cool the pie on a rack.

Makes one 9-inch pie

Pie Pastry

Although the instructions given here are for making pie pastry by hand, it can also be made in a food processor. Just take care to process the ingredients very briefly, pulsing the machine on and off quickly; overprocessing will toughen the dough.

1¼ cups flour
¾ teaspoon salt
4 tablespoons chilled butter, cut into pieces

3 tablespoons chilled vegetable shortening,
   cut into pieces
4 to 5 tablespoons ice water

1. In a large bowl, combine the flour and salt. With a pastry blender or two knives, cut in the butter and the shortening until the mixture resembles coarse crumbs.
2. Sprinkle 4 tablespoons of the ice water over the mixture and toss it with a fork. The dough should be moistened just enough so that it holds together when it is formed into a ball. If necessary, add up to 1 tablespoon more water, drop by drop. Shape the dough into a flat disc, wrap in plastic wrap, and refrigerate for at least 30 minutes, or until well chilled.
3. On a lightly floured surface, roll the dough into a 12-inch circle. Fit the dough into a 9-inch pie pan. Trim the overhang to an even ½ inch all the way around. Fold the overhang over and crimp the dough to form a decorative border. Prick the pastry with a fork. Place the pie shell in the freezer for at least 15 minutes before filling and baking.

Makes one 9-inch crust

Almond-Pecan Shortnin' Bread

Almond-Pecan Shortnin' Bread

Shortnin' bread isn't bread at all, but a rich cookie made with a great deal of short-ening—in this case, butter. Almonds and pecans add interesting texture and flavor to this recipe.

2 sticks (8 ounces) butter	1 cup chopped almonds
⅓ cup (packed) light brown sugar	½ cup chopped pecans
2 cups flour	¼ teaspoon almond extract

1. In a large bowl, cream the butter until softened. Gradually add the brown sugar and continue beating until fluffy. Gradually beat in the flour and blend well. Stir in the almonds, pecans, and almond extract. Shape the dough into a flat disc, wrap in plastic wrap, and refrigerate until firm, about 1 hour.

2. Preheat the oven to 325°.

3. On a lightly floured surface, roll the dough into a 10 x 12½-inch rectangle about ¼ inch thick. Cut the dough into 2½-inch squares and cut each square into two triangles.

4. With a metal spatula, transfer the triangles to ungreased baking sheets and bake for 20 minutes, or until lightly browned. Cool on racks.   *Makes 40 triangles*

DECORATIVE PIE CRUSTS

Here are three easy techniques for adding decorative touches to homemade pies, from a very simple "peek-a-boo" crust to the more complex lattice design.

PEEK-A-BOO PIE

To make a peek-a-boo pie, use small cookie cutters (or aspic cutters) to cut shapes that serve not only as decoration but also as steam vents. Roll out the dough for the top crust as usual and then make the cutouts in the dough before laying it over the filling. Trim the overhang and crimp the border.

APPLIQUE PIE

To make appliqué decorations, roll out the dough for the top crust, lay it over the filling, trim the overhang, and crimp the border as usual. Gather up the scraps of dough and reroll them for the appliqués. For thick appliqués, as shown at left, roll the dough out to at least a ⅜-inch thickness. Then, with a sharp paring knife, cut out shapes, such as pears and leaves. If you do not have faith in your freehand skills with a knife, make a paper pattern first and cut around it. Brush the undersides of the appliqués lightly with water and apply them to the top of the pie before baking.

LATTICE-TOP PIE

To make a pie with a lattice top, prepare enough dough for a two-crust pie. Roll out the dough for the bottom crust, fit it into the pie pan, and trim the overhang to an even ½ inch all the way around. Fill the pie. Using an inverted pie pan as a template, cut out a circle of wax paper. Roll out the dough for the top crust, making it slightly larger than the wax paper circle. Using a knife or a serrated pastry wheel, cut the dough into ½-inch-wide strips.

Place the wax paper circle on a baking sheet. Lay strips of dough (you will need five or six) at 1-inch intervals and parallel to one another over the circle; use the longer pieces for the middle of the pie and the shorter pieces for the edges. Fold every other strip of dough back on itself and place one of the remaining strips of dough across the middle of the circle, at right angles to the first set of strips, and on top of the unfolded strips. Lower the folded strips over the crosswise strip. In the same manner, fold back the strips that are now under the crosswise strip and place another crosswise strip parallel to the first one and 1 inch away from it. Continue to "weave" the dough strips until you have completed the lattice top.

Brush the rim of the pie shell with water. Place the baking sheet on the shell so that the lattice top is aligned with the edges of the pie. Holding the wax paper and baking sheet together, gently slide them out from under the lattice top. Trim the strips even with the rim of the pie, fold the bottom crust overhang in, and crimp.

Strawberry-Rhubarb Fool

A fruit dessert brought to this country by the English, a fool is a simple but delicious combination of fruit purée and whipped cream.

8 stalks of rhubarb (about 1½ pounds),
   cut into 2-inch lengths
¾ cup (packed) dark brown sugar
2 tablespoons butter

2 pints strawberries
1 tablespoon grated orange zest
½ teaspoon orange extract
1½ cups heavy cream

1. In a medium saucepan, cook the rhubarb, brown sugar, and butter over medium-low heat, stirring occasionally, until the rhubarb is tender, about 30 minutes.

2. Meanwhile, in a food processor or blender, purée the strawberries. Place the strawberry purée in a large bowl and set aside.

3. Drain the cooked rhubarb in a strainer or colander. Let the rhubarb cool slightly and then purée in a food processor or blender.

4. Stir the rhubarb purée, the orange zest, and the orange extract into the strawberry purée. Cover and refrigerate until well chilled, about 2 hours.

5. In a medium bowl, beat the cream until soft peaks form. Stir the whipped cream into the fruit purée, cover tightly, and refrigerate for at least 2 hours. Serve the fool in small dessert bowls or parfait glasses.

4 to 6 servings

Southern Banana Pudding

In this homey and comforting Southern dessert, layers of sliced bananas and vanilla wafers are covered with a rich vanilla custard and then topped with meringue.

½ cup (packed) dark brown sugar
2 tablespoons flour
4 cups milk
4 whole eggs plus 4 separated eggs
2 teaspoons vanilla extract

1 package (12 ounces) vanilla wafers
6 medium bananas, cut into ½-inch
   rounds (about 5 cups)
2 tablespoons granulated sugar

1. In the top of a double boiler, combine the brown sugar and flour. Beat in the milk and warm the mixture over medium heat until almost boiling.

2. In a large bowl, beat the 4 whole eggs with the 4 egg yolks. Beat a small amount of the hot milk mixture into the eggs to warm them and then add the warmed eggs to the milk mixture in the double boiler. Cook the custard over boiling water, stirring constantly, until it is thick enough to lightly coat the back of a spoon, 10 to 15 minutes. Stir the vanilla extract into the custard, remove from the heat, and cover the surface with plastic wrap to keep a skin from forming.

3. Preheat the oven to 375°.

4. Line the bottom and sides of a 9 x 12-inch baking pan with the vanilla wafers.

Place a layer of bananas on top. Continue alternating layers of wafers and bananas until all of the ingredients have been used up. Pour the custard over the top layer, spreading it to completely cover the bananas and wafers.

5. In a mixing bowl, beat the egg whites until they form soft peaks. Add the granulated sugar and continue beating until stiff peaks form. Spread the meringue over the pudding and bake for about 12 minutes, or until the meringue has browned. Serve warm or chilled.

12 to 16 servings

Indian Pudding with Sour Cream Topping

In her 1833 book, *The American Frugal Housewife*, Mrs. Child gives these tips for making this venerable New England dessert: "Leave plenty of room [in the pan]; for Indian swells very much. The milk with which you mix it should be merely warm; if it be scalding, the pudding will break to pieces."

PUDDING
2 eggs
5 cups milk
½ cup light unsulphured molasses
⅓ cup maple syrup
½ teaspoon baking soda
½ teaspoon cinnamon
¼ teaspoon ground ginger
1 cup white cornmeal

4 tablespoons butter, softened to
   room temperature
1 cup heavy cream

TOPPING
1 cup sour cream
¼ cup (packed) dark brown sugar
¼ teaspoon cinnamon
½ teaspoon vanilla extract

1. Make the pudding: Preheat the oven to 350°. Heavily butter a deep 2-quart baking or soufflé dish.

2. In a large saucepan, off the heat, whisk the eggs well. Whisk in the milk, molasses, maple syrup, baking soda, cinnamon, and ginger. Bring the mixture almost to a simmer over medium heat, stirring constantly.

3. Add the cornmeal slowly, keeping the mixture at a simmer and stirring constantly. Continue simmering, uncovered and stirring occasionally, until the pudding is thick enough to hold its shape solidly in a spoon, 12 to 15 minutes.

4. Beat in the butter and remove from the heat. Beating constantly, add the heavy cream. Pour the pudding into the prepared baking dish and bake for 1 hour.

5. Reduce the oven temperature to 300° and continue baking for 3 hours longer, or until the pudding is firm (it will still be moist and creamy in the center).

6. Meanwhile, make the topping: In a bowl, combine the sour cream, brown sugar, cinnamon, and vanilla. Refrigerate until ready to serve.

7. Serve the pudding hot or at room temperature with the sour cream topping.

6 to 8 servings

Robert E. Lee Cake

It is said that when the future Mrs. Robert E. Lee offered the Confederate general a piece of this lemony cake, he asked for her hand in marriage.

CAKE
1¾ cups cake flour
1 teaspoon baking powder
¼ teaspoon salt
7 eggs, separated
1⅔ cups granulated sugar
¼ cup lemon juice
1 tablespoon grated lemon zest
½ teaspoon cream of tartar

FILLING
5 egg yolks
4 tablespoons butter, softened
  to room temperature

½ cup granulated sugar
¼ cup lemon juice
1 tablespoon grated lemon zest
2 teaspoons cornstarch

FROSTING
⅓ cup butter, softened to room
  temperature
2½ cups confectioners' sugar
¼ cup lemon juice
1 egg yolk
1 tablespoon grated lemon zest

1. Preheat the oven to 350°. Heavily butter and flour two 9-inch round cake pans.
2. Make the cake: In a small bowl, combine the flour, baking powder, and salt.
3. In a large bowl, beat the egg yolks and granulated sugar until pale and lemon-colored. Beat in the lemon juice and zest. Gradually beat in the flour mixture, beating well after each addition.
4. In a medium bowl, beat the egg whites until frothy. Add the cream of tartar and continue beating until stiff peaks form. Gently fold the beaten egg whites into the batter.
5. Spread the batter evenly in the prepared pans. Bang the pans once or twice on the counter to remove any air pockets. Bake for 25 minutes, or until a toothpick inserted in the center of the cake comes out clean. Let the cakes cool in the pans for 5 minutes, then turn them out onto racks to cool before filling and frosting them.
6. Meanwhile, make the filling: In a medium saucepan, combine the egg yolks, butter, granulated sugar, lemon juice, lemon zest, and cornstarch. Stirring constantly, cook over very low heat until the mixture is thick enough to coat the back of a spoon, 15 to 20 minutes. Scrape the filling into a bowl and let it cool to room temperature.
7. Make the frosting: In a medium bowl, cream the butter until light and fluffy. Beat in half of the confectioners' sugar and then half of the lemon juice. Beat in the remaining sugar and lemon juice. Beat in the egg yolk and lemon zest.
8. Assemble the cake: Cut each cake layer in half horizontally. Place one layer cut-side up and spread about one-third of the lemon filling over it. Put another layer cut-side down on top and spread it with half the remaining filling; repeat with the third layer and the remaining filling. Top with the fourth layer, cut-side down. Spread the frosting over the top and sides of the cake. Chill (to set the frosting) until ready to serve.

Makes one 9-inch layer cake

Robert E. Lee Cake

Politics and dessert may be unlikely partners, yet there are many cakes named for generals and presidents. There is also election cake, which was a New England institution during the 19th century. This raised fruit cake was served to the town legislators on meeting days as a reward for governing the town.

Strawberry-Apricot Shortcake

Strawberry-Apricot Shortcake

Although strawberries are the usual component of this classic American dessert, other fruits also work nicely. Try sliced peaches with raspberry preserves. Or, in the winter, try halved seedless grapes with warm apple jelly.

2 cups flour
⅓ cup granulated sugar
1 tablespoon baking powder
½ teaspoon salt
1 stick (4 ounces) chilled butter,
  cut into pieces

1¼ cups heavy cream
½ cup apricot preserves
1 pint strawberries, halved
1 tablespoon confectioners' sugar
Whole strawberries, for garnish

1. Preheat the oven to 450°. Lightly butter a baking sheet.

2. In a large bowl, combine the flour, sugar, baking powder, and salt. With a pastry blender or two knives, cut in the butter until the mixture resembles coarse meal.

3. Pour in ¾ cup of the cream and blend until a soft dough is formed. Transfer the dough to a lightly floured surface and knead it for about 1 minute, adding a tablespoon or two of flour, if necessary, to keep the dough from sticking.

4. Roll the dough into a circle about ½ inch thick. With a floured plain or scalloped 3-inch round cutter, cut out 6 rounds (you may need to gather the scraps and reroll the dough to get all 6 shortcakes).

5. Bake the shortcakes on the prepared baking sheet for 10 to 12 minutes, or until golden brown. Cool them on a rack.

6. Meanwhile, prepare the fruit: In a small saucepan, stir the apricot preserves over medium-low heat until melted, about 5 minutes. Place the strawberry halves in a bowl, pour the melted preserves on top, and toss the fruit gently to mix.

7. In a small mixing bowl, beat the remaining ½ cup heavy cream with the confectioners' sugar until stiff peaks form.

8. To serve, split the shortcakes in half. Cover the bottom half with the strawberry-apricot mixture and replace the top. Serve with the sweetened whipped cream and garnish with whole strawberries, if desired.   *6 servings*

New Orleans Bread Pudding with Bourbon Sauce

Originally the country cook's solution for using up stale bread as well as cream and eggs, bread pudding is now considered an elegant dessert. This rich version is accented with pecans and accompanied with bourbon sauce.

BREAD PUDDING

1 cup pecans, toasted (see Note) and chopped
½ cup (packed) light brown sugar
4 tablespoons butter, melted
1 teaspoon vanilla extract
1 teaspoon cinnamon
½ teaspoon nutmeg
5 eggs
2 cups milk
1 cup golden raisins
12 slices stale firm-textured white bread,
  cut into cubes (about 6 cups)

PECAN TOPPING

½ cup pecans, toasted (see Note) and chopped
⅓ cup (packed) dark brown sugar
½ teaspoon cinnamon

BOURBON SAUCE

4 tablespoons butter
½ cup (packed) dark brown sugar
1 teaspoon cornstarch
¼ cup heavy cream
1 teaspoon vanilla extract
2 tablespoons bourbon

1. Preheat the oven to 350°. Butter an 8-inch square baking pan.

2. Make the pudding: In a small bowl, combine the pecans, sugar, butter, vanilla, cinnamon, and nutmeg. In a large bowl, beat the eggs until frothy. Add the pecan mixture and blend well. Stir in the milk and raisins.

3. Place the bread cubes in the prepared pan. Pour the egg mixture over them and toss gently until the bread is soaked. Let the pudding sit until the bread has absorbed nearly all of the liquid, about 35 minutes. Stir the mixture once or twice to moisten the bread evenly.

4. Meanwhile, make the topping: In a small bowl, combine the pecans, sugar, and cinnamon. Set aside.

5. Bake the pudding for 25 minutes. Sprinkle the pecan topping over the pudding and continue baking for another 10 minutes, or until the pudding is set and the topping browned.

6. Meanwhile, make the bourbon sauce: In a small saucepan, melt the butter over medium heat. Stir in the sugar and cornstarch, and cook, stirring, until dissolved. Whisk in the cream and vanilla, and continue cooking, stirring, until the sauce thickens slightly, 1 to 2 minutes. Stir in the bourbon and cook, stirring, for another 30 seconds. Remove the sauce from the heat and let it cool slightly.

7. To serve, spoon the pudding out onto plates, then ladle a bit of the bourbon sauce over each serving.   *8 servings*

NOTE: To toast the pecans, place them on an ungreased cookie sheet in a preheated 375° oven for 10 minutes, or until golden.

Key Lime Pie

The uninitiated may be surprised to discover condensed milk among the ingredients for this famous pie, but it is absolutely essential to its authenticity. In pre-refrigeration days in Key West, Florida, where the pie was invented around the turn of the century, cooks had no way to keep milk fresh and used canned instead.

11 graham crackers
2 tablespoons sugar
⅓ cup butter, melted
3 whole eggs plus 3 egg yolks

1 can (14 ounces) sweetened condensed milk
⅔ cup lime juice (about 6 limes)
1 tablespoon grated lime zest
Unsweetened whipped cream, for garnish

1. Preheat the oven to 375°.
2. Make the crust: In a food processor or blender, process the crackers and sugar until the crackers form fine crumbs. Turn the crumb mixture into a bowl, add the melted butter, and blend well.
3. Press the crumb mixture into a 9-inch pie pan to form a crust. Bake for 8 to 10 minutes, or until the crust just begins to color. Let the crust cool before filling it.
4. Lower the oven temperature to 350°.
5. Make the filling: In a bowl, beat the whole eggs and egg yolks together. Whisk in the sweetened condensed milk. Stir in the lime juice and zest.
6. Gently pour the filling into the cooled crust and bake for 10 to 12 minutes, or until just set. Let the pie cool to room temperature and then refrigerate until chilled, 4 to 6 hours. Serve with unsweetened whipped cream, if desired.   *Makes one 9-inch pie*

Chocolate Chip Cookies

The first chocolate chip cookie recipe was created in the 1930s by Ruth Wakefield, owner of the Toll House Inn near Whitman, Massachusetts.

6 tablespoons butter, softened
⅓ cup (packed) dark brown sugar
¼ cup granulated sugar
1 egg, lightly beaten
1 teaspoon vanilla extract

1 cup flour
½ teaspoon baking soda
¾ cup chopped walnuts
1 package (6 ounces) semisweet
  chocolate chips

1. Preheat the oven to 375°. Lightly butter two baking sheets.
2. In a medium bowl, cream the butter. Beat in the brown sugar and then the granulated sugar, beating well after each addition. Beat in the egg and vanilla. Beat in the flour and baking soda. Then stir in the nuts and chocolate chips.
3. Drop the cookie dough by the teaspoon onto the baking sheets, leaving 2 inches of space between the cookies. Bake for about 9 minutes, or until the edges of the cookies just begin to brown. Cool them on a rack.   *Makes about 3 dozen*

Peaches and Cream Ice Cream

If you do not have an ice cream machine, but do have a food processor, use this method: Pour the ice cream mixture into a large metal bowl and place it in the freezer until frozen. Spoon the frozen ice cream into a food processor and process to break up the ice crystals. Stir in the peaches and return the ice cream to the freezer.

2 cups milk
2 whole eggs plus 4 egg yolks, lightly beaten
1 cup (packed) light brown sugar

2 cups heavy cream
1½ teaspoons vanilla extract
1 pound peaches, peeled and finely chopped

1. In the top of a double boiler, combine the milk, whole eggs, egg yolks, and brown sugar. Cook the mixture over medium-high heat, stirring, until the custard coats the back of a spoon, about 10 minutes.

2. Let the custard cool to room temperature and then stir in the heavy cream and vanilla. Chill the custard in the refrigerator for about 2 hours.

3. Pour the custard into the canister of an ice cream maker and freeze according to the manufacturer's instructions. When the ice cream is frozen but still soft, stir in the peaches and continue freezing. Cover the canister with plastic or foil and place it in the freezer for 2 or 3 hours before serving.

Makes about 2 quarts

Wellesley Fudge Cake

In the late 19th century, it was the fad and the fashion among the undergraduates at women's colleges to make fudge over the gaslights in their rooms — generally on the sly and after "lights out." This chocolatey cake from a tea room in Wellesley, Massachusetts, was very likely created in response to the collegiate passion.

CAKE
4 ounces unsweetened chocolate
1¾ cups milk
1 stick (4 ounces) butter, softened to room
    temperature
1½ cups granulated sugar
3 eggs
1 teaspoon vanilla extract
1¾ cups cake flour
¼ cup unsweetened cocoa powder
1 tablespoon baking powder

½ teaspooon salt
1 cup chopped walnuts

FROSTING
4 ounces unsweetened chocolate
1½ sticks (6 ounces) butter, cut into pieces
½ cup unsweetened cocoa powder
5 cups confectioners' sugar, sifted
⅓ cup milk
2 teaspoons vanilla extract
1 teaspoon lemon juice

1. Make the cake: Preheat the oven to 350°. Butter two 8-inch round cake pans and line the bottoms with circles of buttered wax paper.

2. In the top of a double boiler, melt the chocolate in ½ cup of the milk, stirring until smooth. Set aside to cool slightly.

3. In a large bowl, cream the butter and sugar. Beat in the eggs, one at a time, beating well after each addition. Stir in the melted chocolate and vanilla, and blend well.

4. In another bowl, combine the flour, cocoa, baking powder, and salt. Alternating between the two, add the dry ingredients and the remaining 1¼ cups milk to the chocolate mixture, beating well after each addition. Fold in the walnuts.

5. Spread the batter evenly in the prepared pans. Bang the pans once or twice on the counter to remove any air pockets. Bake for 40 minutes, or until a toothpick inserted in the center of the cake comes out clean.

6. Cool the cakes in the pans for 5 minutes. Turn them out onto cake racks and remove the wax paper. Let the layers cool completely before frosting.

7. Make the frosting: In the top of a double boiler, melt the chocolate over hot but not simmering water. Stir in the butter and cocoa, and blend thoroughly.

8. Off the heat, gradually beat in the confectioners' sugar and milk, alternating between the two and blending well after each addition. Beat in the vanilla and lemon juice.

9. Assemble the cake: Spread a generous layer of frosting over one cake layer. Top with the second layer, then frost the top and sides of the cake.

Makes one 8-inch layer cake

Pears come in many different varieties, each with its own unique attributes. Red Bartletts are sweet and beautifully crimson. The small, round Seckel pears, with their olive-colored skin, are ideal for making chutneys and other preserves. Tender, fragrant Comice pears are perfect for eating either on their own or with a fine blue cheese after dinner.

Wellesley Fudge Cake

Pear-Apple Crisp

There is a whole category of fruit desserts that are essentially crustless pies. In crisps (also called crumbles), a buttery crumb topping acts as a top crust. If the crumbs are thoroughly mixed with the fruit, the dessert becomes a Brown Betty. Serve this crisp warm, topped with a scoop of vanilla ice cream.

4 medium Granny Smith apples, unpeeled
   and sliced ½ inch thick
2 firm medium pears, such as Bosc or Bartlett,
   unpeeled and sliced ⅛ inch thick
1 cup chopped walnuts
½ cup fresh breadcrumbs
⅓ cup (packed) dark brown sugar
1 tablespoon lemon juice
½ teaspoon cinnamon

TOPPING
1 cup chopped walnuts
⅔ cup flour
⅓ cup old-fashioned rolled oats
½ cup (packed) dark brown sugar
¼ teaspoon cinnamon
1 stick (4 ounces) butter, melted

1. Preheat the oven to 350°. Butter a shallow 1-quart baking dish.

2. In a large bowl, toss together the apples, pears, walnuts, breadcrumbs, sugar, lemon juice, and cinnamon. Turn the mixture into the prepared baking dish.

3. Make the topping: In a medium bowl, combine the walnuts, flour, oats, sugar, and cinnamon. Add the melted butter and toss with a fork to evenly distribute.

4. Sprinkle the topping over the fruit and bake for 30 minutes, or until the fruit is tender and the topping is browned and crisp.

4 servings

Bourbon-Pecan Pie

This Southern classic tastes especially good served with whipped cream flavored with bourbon and a small amount of sugar, or with Rum-Raisin Ice Cream (below).

Pie Pastry (page 140)
4 tablespoons butter, softened to
    room temperature
⅓ cup (packed) dark brown
    sugar

3 eggs
¾ cup dark corn syrup
2 tablespoons bourbon
1½ cups pecan halves

    1. Make the Pie Pastry.
    2. Preheat the oven to 350°.
    3. In a mixing bowl, cream the butter and sugar. Add the eggs, one at a time, blending well after each addition. Beat in the corn syrup and bourbon until well blended. Stir in the pecans.
    4. Pour the mixture into the pie shell and bake for 40 to 45 minutes, or until the filling has set and is slightly puffed. Cool the pie on a rack before serving.

Makes one 9-inch pie

Rum-Raisin Ice Cream

To save some time, instead of plumping the raisins in rum, cover them with a small amount of boiling water and let them steep for about ten minutes. Then drain the raisins well and soak them in the rum while you prepare the ice cream mixture through the end of Step 2.

¾ cup dark rum
2 cups golden raisins
5 cups heavy cream

1 cup (packed) dark brown sugar
1½ teaspoons vanilla extract

    1. Combine the rum and raisins in a small bowl and set aside for 8 hours, or overnight, to soften the raisins.
    2. In a small saucepan, combine 1 cup of the cream and the sugar, and simmer over low heat, stirring, until the sugar dissolves and small bubbles appear around the edges of the pan, about 5 minutes. Remove the pan from the heat and set aside to cool to room temperature. When the mixture has cooled, stir in the remaining 4 cups cream, the vanilla, raisins, and rum. Refrigerate until chilled, about 2 hours.
    3. Pour the ice cream mixture into the canister of an ice cream maker and freeze according to the manufacturer's instructions (or follow the food processor method described on page 153). Cover the canister with plastic or foil and place in the freezer until the ice cream is firm, 2 to 3 hours.

Makes about 2 quarts

Bourbon-Pecan Pie and Rum-Raisin Ice Cream

PITTERS AND SEEDERS

Blessed with an abundance of fruit, America's early settlers created ingenious gadgets for removing the pits and seeds, especially from small fruits like cherries and raisins. At first their devices were homemade and one-of-a-kind; it was not until the Civil War era that manufacturers began to sell a wide range of cast-iron and steel pitters and seeders, often through mail-order catalogs. Though today raisins come seedless and cherry pitters have been streamlined, collectors still seek out the early devices for their quaintness and inventiveness.

The simplest cherry pitters, or stoners, took only one fruit at a time: a plunger impaled the cherry and pushed out the pit. Another type rubbed several cherries against a ridged wheel.

The name raisin seeder is misleading because the device did not actually seed the raisin but rather mashed the fruit and the tiny seeds simultaneously. This was done by pushing the fruit through coarse wires or small holes. Raisin seeders worked best with softened fruit, and some manufacturers cast "Wet the Raisins" directly onto the device.

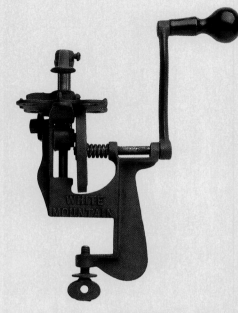

This piston-action raisin seeder was patented c. 1859 by White Mountain.

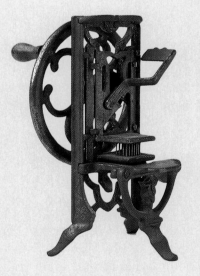

Made in the 1870s by F. A. Walker, this freestanding raisin seeder is only 6½ inches high.

This No. 75 Junior cherry pitter from Pennsylvania separates pit from fruit by means of a ridged "plate."

Handcrafted in fruitwood, this 19th-century English pitter uses a plunge to pit one cherry at a time.

The EZY Raisin Seeder, patented in 1895, has a sinuous pump handle.

The pins on this steel c. 1875-1885 raisin seeder push the raisin through a grid of tiny holes.

This New Hampshire-made cherry pitter could impale two at a time.

This c.1930s-1940s single-cherry pitter works by means of a spring-loaded plunger. The device could be placed on a bottle, which would catch the pits.

Produced in Mount Joy, Pennsylvania, this crank-turned cherry pitter has an unusual horizontal plunger.

Patented in 1863, this freestanding cherry pitter channels the cherries and pits separately.

Steamed Cranberry Pudding with
Orange Hard Sauce

Steamed Cranberry Pudding with Orange Hard Sauce

Because steamed puddings (which are really more like cakes than puddings) are "baked" on a rack in a pot of boiling water, they were a popular dessert with cooks—cowboys among them—who had either limited oven space or no oven at all.

PUDDING
1 stick (4 ounces) butter, softened
    to room temperature
½ cup (packed) dark brown sugar
1 egg, lightly beaten
½ teaspoon orange extract
2 teaspoons grated orange zest
1 cup flour
¼ cup fresh breadcrumbs
2 teaspoons baking powder
½ teaspoon salt
⅔ cup milk

2 cups fresh or frozen cranberries
1 cup mixed dried fruit (about 6 ounces),
    chopped
½ cup chopped walnuts

ORANGE HARD SAUCE
4 tablespoons butter, softened
    to room temperature
¾ cup confectioners' sugar, sifted
2 tablespoons heavy cream
½ teaspoon orange extract
1 teaspoon grated orange zest

1. Make the pudding: In a medium bowl, cream the butter and brown sugar. Beat in the egg, orange extract, and orange zest. In a small bowl, combine the flour, breadcrumbs, baking powder, and salt.

2. Alternating between the two, beat the dry ingredients and the milk into the butter mixture. In a large bowl, combine the cranberries, dried fruit, and walnuts. Fold the fruit-nut mixture into the batter.

3. Spread the batter evenly in an ungreased 1½-quart soufflé dish. Bang the dish lightly once or twice on the counter to remove any air pockets. Cover the dish tightly with foil and tie the foil in place with string. Place the dish on a rack set in a large, deep pot with a cover. Pour in 1 inch of boiling water. Return the water to a boil over high heat. Reduce the heat to low, cover, and steam the pudding until firm, about 2 hours, adding more water as necessary.

4. Meanwhile, make the hard sauce: In a bowl, cream the butter and sugar. Beat in the heavy cream, orange extract, and orange zest. Refrigerate until serving time.

5. Let the pudding cool slightly in the dish for about 10 minutes. Then serve warm with the hard sauce.

6 to 8 servings

Blueberry-Cherry Cobbler

For a different look, roll the biscuit topping into an 8 x 10-inch rectangle and lay it on top of the fruit. Cut several holes in the crust so that steam can escape.

BISCUIT TOPPING
2 cups flour
2 tablespoons sugar
2 teaspoons baking powder
½ teaspoon salt
⅓ cup chilled butter, cut into pieces
½ cup milk

COBBLER FILLING
1 can (17 ounces) dark sweet pitted cherries
3 tablespoons butter, melted
¼ cup sugar
2 tablespoons cornstarch
2½ cups fresh blueberries
2 teaspoons grated lemon zest

1. Preheat the oven to 425°.

2. Make the biscuit topping: In a bowl, combine the flour, sugar, baking powder, and salt. With a pastry blender or two knives, cut the butter into the dry ingredients until the mixture resembles coarse meal. Gradually pour in the milk and mix until a soft dough is formed.

3. Transfer the dough to a lightly floured surface and knead gently several times. Roll the dough into a circle about ½ inch thick. With a floured 2½-inch round cookie cutter, cut out 8 rounds and set aside.

4. Make the filling: Reserving ⅓ cup of the liquid, drain the canned cherries. In a large bowl, combine the reserved cherry liquid, the butter, sugar, and cornstarch. Stir in the cherries, blueberries, and lemon zest.

5. Spread the filling evenly in an 8 x 10 x 2-inch baking dish. Place the circles of dough on top. Bake for 25 minutes, or until the topping is golden. *8 servings*

Cobblers are versatile and can be easily adapted to the amount of time you have and the fruits in season. For a quick cobbler, drop the topping from a spoon onto the filling instead of rolling it out and cutting it; just add a little extra milk to the topping mixture first to loosen the dough enough to be dropped from a spoon. Fresh fruits can be used in almost limitless combinations. Adjust the amount of sugar you add to the sweetness of the fruit and to your own taste.

Orange-Flavored Boston Cream Pie

This custard-filled cake iced with chocolate was once called Parker House Chocolate Pie—in honor of Boston's Parker House hotel (of dinner roll fame) where this classic American dessert was created.

CAKE

1¾ cups cake flour

2 teaspoons baking powder

½ teaspoon salt

⅓ cup butter, softened to room temperature

¾ cup granulated sugar

1 teaspoon vanilla extract

2 eggs

⅓ cup milk

CUSTARD FILLING

1 cup light cream or half-and-half

¼ cup granulated sugar

¼ cup all-purpose flour

⅛ teaspoon salt

1 whole egg plus 1 egg yolk

2 teaspoons grated orange zest

¾ teaspoon orange extract

FROSTING

2 ounces unsweetened chocolate

2 tablespoons butter, softened to room temperature

½ teaspoon orange extract

½ cup (packed) light brown sugar

2 tablespoons light cream or half-and-half

1. Make the cake: Preheat the oven to 350°. Butter and flour two 8-inch round cake pans.

2. In a small bowl, combine the cake flour, baking powder, and salt.

3. In a large bowl, cream the butter and granulated sugar. Beat in the vanilla. Then beat in the eggs, one at a time, beating well after each addition. Alternating between the two, beat in the dry ingredients and the milk.

4. Spread the batter evenly in the prepared pans. Bang the pans once or twice on the counter to remove any air pockets. Bake for 20 minutes, or until a toothpick inserted in the center of the cake comes out clean. Cool the cakes in the pans for 10 minutes and then turn them out onto a rack to cool completely before assembling the cake.

5. Make the custard filling: In a small saucepan, scald the cream. In a medium bowl, combine the granulated sugar, all-purpose flour, and salt. Pour in the hot cream and stir the mixture until smooth.

6. In the top of a double boiler, beat the whole egg and egg yolk together. Slowly pour in the hot cream-flour mixture and cook over boiling water, stirring constantly, until the custard thickens, about 5 minutes. Remove from the heat and stir in the orange zest and extract. Let cool, then cover and refrigerate until ready to use.

7. Make the frosting: In the top of a double boiler, melt the chocolate over hot but not simmering water. Remove the chocolate from the heat and let cool slightly.

8. In a medium bowl, cream the butter and orange extract. Beat in the brown sugar a little at a time, then beat in the cream and the melted chocolate. Continue beating until the frosting is stiff enough to spread.

9. Assemble the cake: Spread the custard filling evenly over one cake layer. Top with the second layer and frost the top of the cake with the chocolate frosting. Chill (to set the frosting) until ready to serve.

Makes one 8-inch layer cake

Almond Tapioca Pudding

Fruits such as raisins, diced bananas, chopped dates, diced peaches, or blackberries make a wonderful addition to this rich, creamy pudding.

3 eggs, separated
1/4 cup quick-cooking tapioca
2 cups milk

1/4 cup sugar
1/4 to 1/2 teaspoon almond extract
1/2 cup sliced almonds, toasted (see Note)

1. In a small bowl, beat the egg yolks lightly with a fork.
2. In a medium saucepan, combine the tapioca, milk, beaten egg yolks, and 2 tablespoons of the sugar. Let the mixture stand for 5 minutes. Stirring constantly, bring the mixture to a boil over medium heat. Remove from the heat.
3. In a medium bowl, beat the egg whites until frothy. Slowly add the remaining 2 tablespoons sugar and continue beating the egg whites until stiff peaks form.
4. Stir in the almond extract. Slowly stir in the egg whites and transfer the pudding to a serving dish. Refrigerate until chilled, 4 to 6 hours. Sprinkle the toasted almonds over the pudding before serving.

4 servings

NOTE: To toast the almonds, place them on an ungreased cookie sheet in a preheated 375° oven for 10 minutes, or until golden.

Fresh Raspberry Frango

A frango may well be the descendant of an early American frozen dessert called a fromage, which, like a frango, was lightened with whipped cream.

3 cups fresh raspberries
1 teaspoon grated lime zest
1 cup light cream or half-and-half

5 egg yolks
1/2 cup honey
2 cups heavy cream

1. In a food processor or blender, purée the raspberries. Stir in the lime zest.
2. In the top of a double boiler, scald the light cream over medium heat. Remove from the heat, cover, and set aside.
3. In a medium bowl, beat the egg yolks and honey together until thick and lemon-colored, 3 to 5 minutes. Gradually whisk in the warm light cream. Pour this mixture back into the pan and cook over low heat until the custard thickens slightly, about 5 minutes; do not let it boil. Pour the custard into a large bowl and let cool to room temperature. Cover and refrigerate until chilled, about 30 minutes.
4. In a bowl, beat the heavy cream until stiff peaks form. Fold the berry purée and the whipped cream into the chilled custard. Spoon the mixture into a 2-quart bowl or mold, cover with plastic wrap or foil, and freeze until semifirm, about 6 hours.

6 servings

Wild Rice Pudding with Dried Fruit

There are few desserts more worthy of the term comfort food than rice pudding. This recipe adds a new twist to the old standby by using wild rice and brown rice in place of the usual white rice.

1½ cups light cream or half-and-half
1½ cups heavy cream
⅓ cup maple syrup
3 whole eggs plus 3 egg yolks
¾ teaspoon vanilla extract
½ teaspoon nutmeg

1 cup mixed dried fruit (about 6 ounces),
   chopped
½ cup golden raisins
1 cup cooked wild rice
1 cup cooked brown rice

1. Preheat the oven to 325°. Butter a shallow 1-quart baking dish.
2. In a large bowl, combine the light cream, heavy cream, maple syrup, whole eggs, egg yolks, vanilla, nutmeg, dried fruit, raisins, wild rice, and brown rice.
3. Turn the mixture into the prepared dish and bake, uncovered, for 35 minutes.
4. Stir the mixture in the baking dish and bake for an additional 5 minutes, or until the custard is set. Serve warm or chilled.

6 servings

Bittersweet Mocha Pudding

When Americans refer to pudding, a smooth, creamy dessert thickened with corn-starch is what they mean. Of course, most of us have only had the commercial packaged variety and would probably be surprised to learn how quick and easy pudding is to make from scratch. Not counting the chilling time, this coffee-flavored chocolate pudding takes only about ten minutes to make.

1¼ cups milk
¾ cup light cream or half-and-half
3 ounces bittersweet chocolate
½ cup sugar
1 tablespoon instant espresso powder

⅛ teaspoon salt
2 tablespoons cornstarch
Sweetened whipped cream and shaved
   bittersweet chocolate, for garnish

1. In a medium saucepan, combine 1 cup of the milk, the light cream, and the chocolate, and cook over low heat until the chocolate has melted. Add the sugar, espresso powder, and salt, and stir to dissolve.
2. Add the remaining ¼ cup milk to the cornstarch and stir to dissolve. Add to the chocolate mixture and cook over medium heat until a few large, slow bubbles erupt on the surface and the pudding has thickened, 2 to 5 minutes.
3. Pour the pudding into individual serving bowls and refrigerate until chilled, about 1 hour. Serve garnished with whipped cream and chocolate shavings.

4 servings

A number of early American fruit desserts seem to have quaint and silly-sounding names, among them slump and grunt. A slump is a dish of cooked fruit topped with dough that is dropped onto the filling by the spoon-ful and baked. A grunt is a fruit dessert in which dumplings are dropped onto a hot berry mixture, then the whole dish is steamed until the dumplings are cooked.

Wild Rice Pudding with Dried Fruit

Gingered Apple Pie

Freshly grated ginger adds zest to this American institution. For an interesting accompaniment, flavor sweetened whipped cream with a small amount of ginger juice (made by squeezing grated ginger in a square of cheesecloth).

Two-Crust Pastry with Ginger (below)
½ cup (packed) dark brown sugar
1 tablespoon grated fresh ginger
1 teaspoon cinnamon
½ teaspoon nutmeg

¼ cup fresh breadcrumbs
3 large Granny Smith apples, unpeeled and
*   cut into ⅛-inch wedges (about 6 cups)*
2½ tablespoons lemon juice
1 egg, beaten

The first pumpkin "pie" was actually a stuffed, baked pumpkin. The Pilgrims would fill a pumpkin with a heavily spiced mixture of meat, apples or other fruit, sugar, and butter, then bury the pumpkin in the hot ashes of the cooking fire. Once cooked, the pumpkin was sliced and served with the filling.

1. Make the Two-Crust Pastry with Ginger.
2. Preheat the oven to 375°.
3. On a lightly floured surface, roll one disc of dough into a 12-inch circle and fit it into a 9-inch pie pan, letting the extra dough hang over the edges. Prick the pastry with a fork. Place the pie shell in the freezer while you prepare the filling.
4. In a large bowl, combine the sugar, fresh ginger, cinnamon, nutmeg, and breadcrumbs. Add the apples and lemon juice, and toss gently. Mound the filling in the pie shell.
5. Roll the remaining disc of dough into a 10-inch circle and place it on top of the filling. Trim the overhang to an even ½ inch all the way around. Fold the overhang in over the top crust, crimping to seal. Cut steam vents in the top crust and brush the crust with the beaten egg. Bake for 50 minutes, or until the crust is golden brown. Serve warm or at room temperature.

Makes one 9-inch pie

Two-Crust Pastry with Ginger

For a decorative touch, roll out any scraps of dough left over after you trim the overhang (see Step 5, above) and cut out decorative shapes, such as an apple and two leaves. Brush the cut-outs lightly with water and press them onto the top crust.

2½ cups flour
1½ teaspoons salt
½ teaspoon ground ginger

1 stick (4 ounces) chilled butter, cut into pieces
⅓ cup chilled vegetable shortening
About 5 tablespoons ice water

1. In a large bowl, combine the flour, salt, and ginger.
2. With a pastry blender or two knives, cut in the butter and the shortening until the mixture resembles coarse meal. Sprinkle 5 tablespoons of ice water over the mixture and toss it with a fork. Add more water if necessary; the dough should be barely moistened, just enough so that it can be gathered or shaped into a ball. Divide the dough in half, press each half into a flat disc shape, wrap in plastic wrap, and refrigerate for at least 30 minutes.

Makes a double crust for a 9-inch pie

Poached Pears with Strawberry Sauce

Poached Pears with Strawberry Sauce

In order to make these elegant-looking poached pears easier to eat, they are cored from the bottom before they are cooked. If you are in a rush, the pears can be poached uncored, although they may take twice as long to cook.

6 Bosc pears with stems
Juice from half a lemon
5 cups cranberry juice, apple cider,
   or apple juice
1 teaspoon coarsely chopped lemon zest

2 packages (10 ounces each) frozen strawberries
   in light syrup, thawed
3 tablespoons rum or bourbon (optional)
Fresh mint sprigs, for garnish
Whipped cream or vanilla ice cream (optional)

1. Peel the pears, leaving the stems intact. Rub the fruit with lemon juice to prevent browning. With an apple corer or vegetable peeler, core the pears from the bottom, coring only halfway up the pear. If some of the pears do not stand upright, take a small slice off the bottom so they will stand straight.

2. Place the pears upright in a 3-quart saucepan and add the cranberry juice. Add the lemon zest and bring to a boil. Reduce the heat to medium-low, cover, and simmer until the pears are tender but firm, about 10 minutes. With a slotted spoon, remove the pears to a plate, cover, and refrigerate until serving time.

3. In a food processor or blender, purée the strawberries. Blend in the rum or bourbon (if using). Pour the sauce into a bowl and refrigerate until serving time.

4. Spoon about ¼ cup of the strawberry sauce onto each of six dessert plates, stand a pear in the center, garnish with mint, and serve with whipped cream or ice cream, if desired.   *6 servings*

FESTIVE DRINKS

ARTILLERY PUNCH

Powerful libations such as artillery punch have been popular as long as there have been artillery regiments. To make this punch, in a medium bowl, combine 2 cups whole strawberries, 1 orange (sliced), ½ pineapple (cut into chunks), 2 cups dark rum, and 2 cups bourbon. Let the fruit macerate overnight in the refrigerator. Pour the mixture into a punch bowl. Add 3 cups chilled sparkling cider, 1 bottle chilled demi-sec or brut champagne, and a block of ice.   *Makes about 3 quarts*

STRAWBERRY SANGAREE

Popular in colonial America, sangaree takes its name from the French word *sang*, meaning "blood," and, indeed, a sangaree is always deep red, usually from the addition of red wine. This strawberry sangaree is nonalcoholic and gets its color from cranberry juice and strawberries, but red wine can be added to taste, if desired. To make this recipe: In a pitcher, combine 4 cups chilled cranberry juice, 2 cups crushed strawberries, and 2 tablespoons lemon juice. Add 2 cups chilled seltzer water and stir to combine. Pour the sangaree into individual glasses and, if desired, garnish each glass with a whole strawberry.

Makes about 8 cups

FROZEN LIME PUNCH

In the 19th century, an ice or sherbet mixed with liquor was often served to clear the palate after a main course. This frozen punch also makes a fine warm-weather cocktail or a refreshing dessert. To prepare it: Let 2 pints lime sherbet soften slightly, then scoop the sherbet into a mixing bowl. Beat in ⅔ to 1 cup light rum (or to taste). If the mixture seems too sweet, add lime juice. Pour the punch into individual glasses and garnish each with a lime slice. *Makes about 5 cups*

RUM POSSET

Popular from the 15th to the 19th century, but rarely drunk today, a posset (from the Middle English *possot*) is a drink of sweetened hot milk to which wine or liquor is added. This recipe includes cream and rum: In the top of a double boiler, mix together 10 beaten egg yolks, 3 cups heavy cream, ¼ cup (packed) dark brown sugar, and ½ teaspoon nutmeg; stir constantly until the custard lightly coats the back of a spoon, 15 to 20 minutes. Stir in ½ cup dark rum and serve the posset warm. *Makes about 6 cups*

For eggnog, chill the mixture, then fold in 4 egg whites that have been beaten until stiff. Refrigerate.

Photography Credits

All photos by Steven Mays, except the following: Pages 14, 24, 25, 36, 37, 42, 43, 68, 69, 72, 76, 77, 84, 85, 90, 91, 96, 97, 104, 105, 110, 111, 118, 119, 144, 145, 150, 151, 158, 159, 162, 163: Rob Whitcomb. Pages 16, 80-81: Alan Shortall. Pages 22-23, 98-99, 112-113, 168-169: Stephen Donelian. Page 45: Jerry Simpson. Pages 122-123: all photos from the collection of the Minnesota Historical Society: top row (far left) and bottom row (far left): photographed by Gordon R. Sommers; top row (second from left and far right) and bottom row (far right): photographed by Monroe Killy.

Prop Credits

The Editors would like to thank the following for their courtesy in lending items for photography. Items not listed below are privately owned. **Cover**: Bennington plates, fruit compote, and ladle—Pantry and Hearth/Gail Lettick Collection, NYC; iron candlesticks—Zona, NYC; wine glasses—Pottery Barn, NYC. **Page 8**: soup tureen and soup bowls—Gear, NYC; wallcovering, "Elizabeth Cobb," ivory, blue, and red—Stroheim & Romann's The American Collection, Long Island City, NY; table—Evergreen Antiques, NYC; cutting board—Pottery Barn, NYC. **Page 10**: sweet corn sign—Judith and James Milne/American Country Antiques, NYC. **Page 13**: table—Judith and James Milne/American Country Antiques, NYC; linens—Gear, NYC. **Page 15**: wooden bowl and checked napkin—Watermelon Patch, Manhasset, NY. **Pages 18-19**: wooden bowl with leeks, basket with tomatoes, spoon, and red and blue napkin—Zona, NYC; yellow bowl—Frank McIntosh at Henri Bendel, NYC; bench—Origin, NYC; blue footstool—Judith and James Milne/American Country Antiques, NYC. **Pages 20-21**: bowls—Simon Pearce, NYC; napkins—Frank McIntosh at Henri Bendel, NYC; cutlery container—Judith and James Milne/American Country Antiques, NYC. **Pages 22-23**: Top shelf, left to right: "Cranshaw Melon" with green leaf dish, earthenware—Eigen Arts, NYC; individual "fish" covered soup—Wolfman-Gold & Good Company, NYC; majolica "Melon" individual tureen—Mottahedeh, NYC; individual "pheasant" covered soup—Wolfman-Gold & Good Company; "White Rabbit" with ladle and liner—The Haldon Group, Irving, TX; "Sugar Melon" with green dish, and red and green "Cabbage" tureen—Eigen Arts. Middle shelf, left to right: "Acorn Squash," earthenware—Eigen Arts; "Gourmet" marmite, oven-to-table—Royal Worcester, NYC; "Rabbit" tureen, porcelain—Mottahedeh; "Basketweave/Vegetable" tureen with liner—Fitz & Floyd, Dallas, TX; individual covered "Pumpkin" soup bowl—Fitz & Floyd; "Gainsborough," imperial earthenware—Spode, NYC; individual covered "Hen" soup bowl—Wolfman-Gold & Good Company. Bottom shelf, left to right: "Cornelia" tureen with liner, English ironstone—Mottahedeh; pink, majolica "Cabbage" covered bowl with rabbit—Mottahedeh; "Confection" tureen with liner, pottery—Presentense, available thru Palmer Smith Linens, NYC; individual "Lettuce" tureen—Mottahedeh; "Blue Italian" tureen with liner, imperial earthenware—Spode. **Pages 24-25**: jars—Linda Mason, Watermelon Patch, Manhasset, NY; tiles—Country Floors, NYC. **Pages 26-27**: flatware, wooden salad bowls, and yellow, blue, and black napkin—Zona, NYC; pottery bowl and underplate—Origin, NYC; glass—Gear, NYC; brown napkin—Frank McIntosh at Henri Bendel, NYC. **Page 29**: spoon and quilt—Judith and James Milne/American Country Antiques, NYC; table—Evergreen Antiques, NYC. **Pages 32-33**: spice tins, baking powder tin, cookie tin, asparagus sign, jam pot, and butter dish—collection of Bonnie J. Slotnick, NYC; rolling pin—Funchie, Bunkers, Gaks and Gleeks, NYC. **Pages 40-41**: large blue and white ironstone platter, square white porcelain bowl, and white lace tea cloth—Vito Giallo Antiques, NYC; paisley Scottish woven runner—Laura Fisher/Antique Quilts & Americana, NYC; Portuguese painted sideboard—Cobweb, NYC. **Pages 46-47**: "Harlequin" tiles—Country Floors, NYC; flatware and dinner plate—Mayhew, NYC. **Page 49**: early bandanna and embroidered state flower map—Laura Fisher/Antique Quilts and Americana, NYC; flatware—Vito Giallo Antiques, NYC. **Page 51**: baking powder tin—collection of Bonnie J. Slotnick, NYC; kitchen towel—Watermelon Patch, Manhasset, NY. **Pages 52-53**: menu created and prepared by Alice Ross, food historian; photographed at the Alice Ross Hearth Studio, Inc., Smithtown, NY. **Page 57**: linen embroidered lace tablecloth—Laura Fisher/Antique Quilts & Americana, NYC; water and wine goblets and "Georgetown" dinner and salad plates—Gear, NYC; napkin—Vito Giallo Antiques, NYC. **Page 58**: flatware—Vito Giallo Antiques, NYC. **Page 61**: tiles—Country Floors, NYC. **Page 62**: basket—Conran's, NYC; table—Origin, NYC. **Page 65**: wallcovering, "Cornflower Resist," Society for the Preservation of New England Antiquities, reproduction—Brunschwig & Fils, Inc., NYC; table—Pierre Deux, NYC; candlestick (center), bowl with mixed fruits, porringer with okra, tankard, and salt shaker—Wilton Armetale, NYC. **Pages 66-67**: casseroles, plates, pitcher, glasses, and tin art—

Pan American Phoenix, NYC; table—Americana West, NYC. **Page 71**: table and chair—Daniel Mack Rustic Furniture, NYC. **Pages 74-75**: tiles—Nemo Tile, NYC. **Pages 76-77**: fabrics—Watermelon Patch, Manhasset, NY. **Pages 82-83**: glasses, casserole, salad bowl, radish bowl, lime wedge bowl, and avocado bowl—Amigo Country, NYC; soup plate—Pottery Barn, NYC; blanket—Common Ground, NYC. **Page 86**: platter—Origin, NYC. **Page 89**: tiles—Country Floors, NYC; table, plates, and bowls—Cobweb, NYC. **Pages 92-93**: table and chair—Florentine Craftsman, Inc., Long Island City, NY; salad plates, pitcher, and glass—Williams-Sonoma, NYC. **Page 97**: chopper—collection of Bonnie J. Slotnick, NYC. **Pages 98-99**: all edible flowers courtesy of and available from Jay North/Paradise Farms, Summerland, CA. **Pages 100-101**: striped napkins—Sweet Nellie, NYC. **Page 102**: calico fabric—Laura Fisher/Antique Quilts

& Americana, NYC. **Page 106**: storage jar—Conran's, NYC; terra-cotta bowl—Pottery Barn, NYC. **Page 124**: Top shelf: napkin—Conran's, NYC. Bottom two shelves: basket and napkins—Pottery Barn, NYC. **Page 138**: decorated tiles—Farley Tiles, Brooklyn, NY; butter dish—collection of Bonnie J. Slotnick, NYC; sugar and flour canisters and napkin—Conran's, NYC; milk jug and rolling pin—Pottery Barn, NYC. **Page 146**: tumblers—Waterford Crystal, NYC; flatware—Buccellati, NYC. **Pages 148-149**: painted blue surface—Bette Blau, NYC. **Page 150**: wallcovering, pattern #82-294-1—Katzenbach & Warren, Inc., NYC. **Page 151**: cookie tin—collection of Bonnie J. Slotnick, NYC. **Pages 152-153**: ice cream dishes, spoons, and crystal vase—James II Galleries, NYC. **Pages 156-157**: dessert plates, glasses with ice cream, silver flatware, coffeepot, liqueur bottles, apéritif glasses, and green glass bowl—James II

Galleries, NYC; vase—Baccarat, NYC; fruit compote and silver tray—Thaxton's, NYC. **Pages 158-159**: cherry pitters from the collection of Donald G. Long, Belle Mead, NJ; raisin seeders from the collection of Paul Neuman and Stacey Bogdonoff, NYC. **Page 160**: bowls—Watermelon Patch, Manhasset, NY; napkin—Platypus, NYC; table—Primrose Lane, Manhasset, NY. **Page 164**: napkin—Frank McIntosh at Henri Bendel, NYC. **Page 167**: dishes—Mottahedeh, NYC; table—Evergreen Antiques, NYC; spoon—Buccellati, NYC. **Page 168**: Top: wallcovering, "Williamsburg Apples"—Katzenbach & Warren, Inc., NYC. Bottom: glasses and faience bowl and plate—Mediterranean Shop, NYC. **Page 169**: Top: glassware, chrome tray, flamingos, and Fiestaware bowl and vase—Mood Indigo, NYC. Bottom: wallcovering, "Stencil Flowers"—Katzenbach & Warren, Inc., NYC.

Index

G

German potato salad, hot, 97
gingered apple pie, 166
grapefruit
   avocado and grapefruit salad with
      poppy-seed dressing, 100
green beans, *see* beans, fresh
green chili, New Mexico, 84
green rice, 108
grillades and grits, 50
grits
   grillades and grits, 50
   grits and Swiss cheese casserole,
      120
   sesame-coated fried grits, 108
gumbo, chicken and sausage, 74

H

ham, country, about, 45
ham and seafood jambalaya, 79
Hangtown fry, 58
hash, red flannel, 48
hashed brown potatoes, 118
hearth cooking, about, 52-55
   recipes, 54-55
herbs, glossary of, 80-81
hominy
   hominy baked with cream and
      Cheddar, 88
   posole, 82
hoppin' John, 114

I

ice cream
   fresh raspberry frango, 163
   peaches and cream ice cream,
      153
   rum-raisin ice cream, 157
Indian pudding with sour cream
   topping, 145

J

jambalaya, ham and seafood, 79
Joe Booker stew, 69
juniper berry, about, 80

K

Kentucky burgoo, 72
key lime pie, 151

L

lamb: American lamb stew, 85
lattice-top pie, 142-143
leeks: potato-leek soup, 15
lemon balm, *see* balm
lemon chess pie, 140
lime gelatin salad, fresh, 91
Louisiana maque choux, 96

M

macaroni, baked, with three cheeses, 64
mace, about, 80
maque choux, Louisiana, 96
marjoram, about, 81
Maryland crab cakes, 47
meat, *see specific types*
meat loaf: country meat loaf with
      carrots, 36
mint
   pan-fried trout with mint and bacon,
      35
   peas with fresh mint, 97
mocha pudding, bittersweet, 165
monkey bread, sweet potato, 126
muddle, red snapper, 84
mushrooms: double-mushroom soup, 14

N

New England boiled dinner, 37
New Mexico green chili, 84
New Orleans bread pudding with
      bourbon sauce, 150
noodles
   baked macaroni with three cheeses,
      64
   chicken-corn soup with, 28

O

okra
   chicken and sausage gumbo, 74
   Kentucky burgoo, 72
onions
   cucumber-onion salad, 90
   Vidalia onion pie with bacon and
      cheese, 94
oregano, about, 81
oysters
   ham and seafood jambalaya, 79
   Hangtown fry, 58

P

pancakes, potato-cheese, with scallions,
      110
pasta, *see* noodles
pastry
   decorative pie crusts, 142-143
   pie pastry, 140
   two-crust pastry with ginger, 166
peaches and cream ice cream, 153
peanuts: Virginia peanut soup, 24
pears
   pear-apple crisp, 155
   poached pears with strawberry sauce,
      167
peas, dried, about, 112-113
   yellow split pea, yam, and carrot
      soup, 20
peas, fresh
   fresh pea soup, 21
   peas and cheese salad, 105
   peas with fresh mint, 97
pecans: bourbon-pecan pie, 157
peek-a-boo pie, 142-143
Pennsylvania-German fried tomatoes,
      102
pie crust, *see* pastry
pies and tarts, savory
   chicken pot pie in a cheese crust, 32
   Vidalia onion pie with bacon and
      cheese, 94
pies and tarts, sweet
   bourbon-pecan pie, 157
   gingered apple pie, 166
   key lime pie, 151
   lemon chess pie, 140
pilau, chicken and shrimp, 68
pine bark stew, 70
pine nuts: pumpkin-pine nut bread, 137
pitters, cherry, 158-159
popovers, nut, 133
poppy-seed dressing, avocado and
      grapefruit salad with, 100
pork
   barbecued spareribs with orange
      sauce, 48
   New Mexico green chili, 84
   pork chops with sausage-apple
      stuffing, 60
   posole, 82

First printing
Published simultaneously in Canada
School and library distribution by Silver Burdett Company,
Morristown, New Jersey

TIME-LIFE is a trademark of Time Incorporated U.S.A.

Production by Giga Communications, Inc.
Printed in U.S.A.

Library of Congress Cataloging-in-Publication Data

Country cooking.
(American country)
Includes index.
1. Cookery, American.   I. Time-Life Books.   II. Series.
TX715.C86125   1989   641.5973   88-36270
ISBN 0-8094-6775-5
ISBN 0-8094-6776-3 (lib. bdg.)

American Country was created by Rebus, Inc., and published by Time-Life Books.

REBUS, INC.

Publisher: RODNEY FRIEDMAN • Editor: MARYA DALRYMPLE
Executive Editor: RACHEL D. CARLEY • Managing Editor: BRENDA SAVARD • Food Editor: KATE SLATE
Associate Editor: SARA COLLINS MEDINA • Copy Editors: MARSHA LUTCH LLOYD, HELEN SCOTT-HARMAN
Writers: JUDITH CRESSY, ROSEMARY G. RENNICKE
Freelance Writers: MINDY HEIFERLING, ANNE E. MAGRUDER, REGINA SCHRAMBLING
Design Editors: NANCY MERNIT, CATHRYN SCHWING
Test Kitchen Director: GRACE YOUNG • Freelance Food Stylists: SIDNEY BURSTEIN, KAREN HATT
Editor, The Country Letter: BONNIE J. SLOTNICK
Editorial Assistant: SANTHA CASSELL • Contributing Editor: ANNE MOFFAT

Art Director: JUDITH HENRY • Associate Art Director: SARA REYNOLDS
Designers: AMY BERNIKER, TIMOTHY JEFFS
Photographer: STEVEN MAYS • Photo Editor: SUE ISRAEL
Photo Assistant: ROB WHITCOMB • Freelance Photographers: STEPHEN DONELIAN, ALAN SHORTALL
Freelance Photo Stylists: ADRIENNE ABSECK, BETTE BLAU, VALORIE FISHER,
DENISE L. ROWLEY, DEE SHAPIRO

Series Consultants: BOB CAHN, HELAINE W. FENDELMAN, LINDA C. FRANKLIN, GLORIA GALE,
KATHLEEN EAGEN JOHNSON, JUNE SPRIGG, CLAIRE WHITCOMB

Time-Life Books Inc. is a wholly owned subsidiary of TIME INCORPORATED.

FOUNDER: HENRY R. LUCE 1898-1967

Editor-in-Chief: JASON McMANUS • Chairman and Chief Executive Officer: J. RICHARD MUNRO
President and Chief Operating Officer: N. J. NICHOLAS JR. • Editorial Director: RICHARD B. STOLLEY
Executive Vice President, Books: KELSO F. SUTTON • Vice President, Books: PAUL V. McLAUGHLIN

TIME-LIFE BOOKS INC.

Editor: GEORGE CONSTABLE • Executive Editor: ELLEN PHILLIPS
Director of Design: LOUIS KLEIN • Director of Editorial Resources: PHYLLIS K. WISE
Editorial Board: RUSSELL B. ADAMS JR., DALE M. BROWN, ROBERTA CONLAN, THOMAS H. FLAHERTY,
LEE HASSIG, DONIA ANN STEELE, ROSALIND STUBENBERG
Director of Photography and Research: JOHN CONRAD WEISER
Assistant Director of Editorial Resources: ELISE RITTER GIBSON

President: CHRISTOPHER T. LINEN • Chief Operating Officer: JOHN M. FAHEY JR.
Senior Vice Presidents: ROBERT M. DeSENA, JAMES L. MERCER, PAUL R. STEWART
Vice Presidents: STEPHEN L. BAIR, RALPH J. CUOMO, NEAL GOFF, STEPHEN L. GOLDSTEIN,
JUANITA T. JAMES, CAROL KAPLAN, SUSAN J. MARUYAMA, ROBERT H. SMITH, JOSEPH J. WARD
Director of Production Services: ROBERT J. PASSANTINO
Supervisor of Quality Control: JAMES KING

For information about any Time-Life book please call 1-800-621-7026, or write:
Reader Information, Time-Life Customer Service
P.O. Box C-32068, Richmond, Virginia 23261-2068

Time-Life Books Inc. offers a wide range of fine recordings, including a Rock 'n' Roll Era series.
For subscription information, call 1-800-621-7026, or write TIME-LIFE MUSIC,
P.O. Box C-32068, Richmond, Virginia 23261-2068.